100 YEARS OF SOCIAL HOUSING IN SOMERS TOWN

EDITORIAL

Cooper's Lane Estate, Ossulston Estate, Sidney Estate, Aldenham and Wolcott House, Churchway Estate, Mayford Estate, Goldington Street Estate, Godwin and Crowndale Estate:

These are just a few of the names of estates provided by the council in one guise or another or by housing associations in the small bounded area of Somers Town.
This is social housing and Somers Town has plenty of it.

Each of these developments comes with a rich history of how it came to be, how it was designed, who lived within it, what aspiration it was to embody.

The history of social housing finds a special site in Somers Town, with the trailblazing efforts of Basil Jellicoe on the Sidney Estate and the bold ambitions of council-directed architects, from those at the London County Council, who brought Levita House into being in the 1920s, to those in Camden Council, who designed Oakshott Court in the 1960s.

Somers Town was a testing ground for what might be possible in terms of the dignity of life if slums were replaced not just by homes but by beautiful homes and community facilities. It was a place where modernism from the European continent was allowed to develop further some experimental forms for the well-being of those who might never normally get to enjoy its dimensions and its architectural philosophy. It was a place where it was understood that housing was never on its own enough.

This second issue of our Somers Town journal offers some glimpses into the history of social housing in Somers Town. It is not comprehensive, but rather a start at excavating a model set of practices, some heroic efforts to bring improvements to those who are often worn down and made to least expect them.

It opens a window onto what existed before the provision of social housing and details the legislative changes that ushered various waves of housing into existence. It explores some of the early forms that replaced the chaotic misery of the slums and observes how a golden age of town planning and architectural design came about, though not simply as some natural development, but rather as a conscious act of policy on the basis of a faith in what was deserved by all as a right.

As part of this story are also the acts of taking power into their own hands on the part of those – rent strikers or squatters – who rebelled in order to try to bring about what they perceived as a more just or equitable situation. Like many histories that span the twentieth century, this one slips into a dark mode as an era of cut backs and decay arises. Our history details how a community attempted to make itself comfortable in uncomfortable times, when the very belief in social housing was under attack from various quarters and there was a rush to sell off whatever could be sold off, as another faith – the belief in the market – came to reign supreme.

Some say we are now entering a new golden age of social housing – with the 94-home Goldsmith Street council housing development in Norwich winning the 2019 Royal Institute of British Architects' Stirling Prize. If this is the case, then surely there is no greater argument for Somers Town to have a museum, an open-air one, as much as an interior space, because here we have every single era of social housing represented and so it may be a pattern book for the future too.

What social housing means, whether it might be funded by the private sector or used as a trade-off, whether councils might build multi-storey private developments slap in the middle of social housing's only park, who lives in social housing and has the right to keep it within the family: all this is up for debate in our tiny local area and so we have provided a very contemporary glossary to help us get a handle on the lexicon of the present. We will need it.

Professor Esther Leslie,
Author and Academic

SOMERS TOWN

A SOCIAL LABORATORY

BY JOE KERR

When I was asked a while ago to curate an architectural walking tour for the Wellcome Trust on the theme of Buildings and Health, I knew immediately that I wanted that walk to come to Somers Town. Indeed, the subject could not have fitted Somers Town more perfectly, as this is an area in which so many architectural and institutional experiments have been conducted to try to improve the health of its residents, that I think of it as a vast, real-life laboratory for testing modern ideas about human health and wellbeing.

In fact, I don't think Somers Town is appreciated as much as it deserves to be, as perhaps the densest concentration of social architecture in London. Hospitals and health buildings, schools, community facilities and, above all else, social housing constitute virtually the entire building stock of this extraordinary little enclave. Indeed, so extensive is the social housing stock, constructed relentlessly across the entire twentieth century, that the area virtually constitutes an open-air museum of progressive housing ideas.

This architectural legacy alone makes the area of particular interest - but not exceptional, for there are comparable areas of the East End, Whitechapel for instance, that were subjected to equally intensive and comprehensive redevelopment with social housing.

What makes the case of Somers Town unique is its location, situated as it is right on the fringes of central London, separated on the south side from Bloomsbury merely by the width of the Euston Road, which has always operated as a kind of fire break between privilege and poverty.

This juxtaposition of an area characterised by poverty, overcrowding and ill-health with a district inhabited by an educated and liberal-minded elite has had a profound effect on both communities, for it was so often progressively-minded professionals living in the terraces and squares of Bloomsbury who focussed their ambitions on their underprivileged neighbours in Somers Town. Doctors, artists, architects and politicians alike focussed their new and often untested theories on a working-class community that had little choice in the matter.

Indeed, in the instance of social housing, this relationship is established from the very beginning: Goldington Buildings, a rather grand tenement block built by the newly-formed St. Pancras Borough Council on the north eastern fringe of Somers Town, has always been associated with George Bernard Shaw, borough councillor and resident of Fitzroy Square.

It is telling perhaps that the Council quickly established itself on the south side of the Euston Road, from where the so-called "red flag borough" embarked on the most ambitious of all council housing programmes after 1945, largely directed at its citizens north of the Euston Rd.

This relationship between the two districts was always fraught with tension, which was inevitable given the paternalistic manner in which the educated elite imposed their beliefs and aspirations on the passive subjects of their experiments.

But there was also a darker side to the story as well, as the desire to "improve" the lower orders amongst some of the most influential professional activists was tainted by the shadow of eugenics, a shameful ingredient in the contemporary discourse of social reform that has only been properly exposed in recent years.

However, at its best, the impulse of privileged campaigners to ameliorate the conditions of those less well off, left an impressive and laudable legacy on the housing stock of an area that had become synonymous with ill-health and deprivation. The wonderful agitprop campaigns by the St. Pancras House Improvement Society, in which large models of fleas and cockroaches were burnt to dramatise the benefits of replacing slum housing, are vivid symbols of the extraordinary achievements of a dedicated group of professional pioneers.

Somers Town also embodies the best of municipal reform, from the LCC's massive and towering Ossulston Street Estate, with its alien echoes of the great superblocks of Red Vienna, through to the restrained but convincing efforts of the fabled Camden Architects' Department at Oakshott Court, built almost at the end of the era of council housing.

Somers Town also bears witness to the decline and disillusion in the whole concept of mass housing construction, with the last few remaining streets of the former Brewers estate along Charrington Street, a testimony to the housing activists who saved them from destruction at the hands of the GLC.

In the decades since then, the area has been tainted by the general antipathy that has been generated towards social housing and its tenancy, but has until now remained largely intact as a concentrated enclave of affordable, high-density housing, even remaining impervious in large part to the regeneration and gentrification that has transformed comparable communities in other inner London districts.

However, the signs for the immediate future are ominous, as plans for luxury housing and for high end medical facilities nibble at the fringes, and as schools and housing blocks fall under threat of demolition to allow for densification and for the dilution of the demographic of social housing tenancies.

Right now it is still possible to look back on the achievements of a century and more of housing reform in Somers Town and to applaud the consequences.

I wish it were possible to legislate to conserve the particular built legacy of this intriguing place, for it is as significant an architectural expression of its era as the squares of Bloomsbury are of an earlier age.

But it is impossible to imagine that the ambitions and dreams enshrined in the fabric of Somers Town will ever be valued sufficiently to merit preserving.

JOE KERR IS AN ACADEMIC AT THE ROYAL COLLEGE OF ART, FORMER RESIDENT OF SOMERS TOWN

Photos of various estates including Grafton House, Levita House Oakshott Court and St. Pancras Housing courtyards by Iris Watson using a Instax camera.

NELLY AND DANNY, EX-DRIVING INSTRUCTOR, ST PANCRAS FLATS

Nelly was born 96 years ago in Stibbington Street in what is now known as a slum. She remembers families living in one room. They are in front of the drying posts decorated with bird finials by Gilbert Bayes as 'Art in everyday life' (replicas) outside the Basil Jellicoe Hall, where Nelly wed during the war.
She worked in the censor's office as part of the war effort, but won't reveal what she read to this day. Her family all live in the area, as does Danny, who is a distant cousin.
She now lives on the Regent Park estate, but the family meet each week.

Photo by Diana Foster

GEORGE, EX-MARKET TRADER AND TAXI DRIVER, WITH JOHN, HIS BROTHER, OUTSIDE ST. JOSEPH'S FLATS

George, Nelly's brother, was born in Stibbington Street and moved to St. Joseph's at the age of three, some 80 years ago. He found an picture of himself in a publicity photograph in the St. Pancras Archives. He still lives in the area, having moved with his young family to council block Oakshott shortly after it was built, where he now lives.
In the distance is his sister-in-law, Doreen, who lives in the St. Pancras flats.
Photo by Diana Foster

DANNY AND RON, RETIRED PLUMBER, ST. RICHARD'S FLATS

Danny and Ron are friends and both have lived in the area for a long time. They meet at Pinner cafe several times a week - the owners give Dolly, the dog, a sausage. Ron used to live in Levita House, and used to run his own plumbing firm, and contracted for St. Pancras Housing, now Origin. He remembers the Gilbert Bayes finials that used to decorate the drying posts. being stored in the workshop. Danny is Chair of the Tenants Association, who are shocked at some of the high rents being charged.
Photo by John Carroll

BEGINNINGS

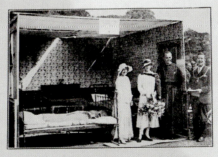

NORTH ST. PANCRAS

AFFAIRS in North St. Pancras are making steady progress, and it is hoped t building of the first block of flats in Kentish Town can be commenced quit next year.

The Group has held several large meetings in Hampstead, in particular an "At given by Lady Pentland, at the Hampstead Town Hall, when about 300 people were to see the film "Paradox Cit to hear a very representative of speakers, including Lord hulme, Sir Humphrey R and Father Jellicoe.

A really enjoyable Garde opened by H.R.H. Prince Countess of Athlone, was July 14 in the grounds Elms," Hampstead Heath lent by Mrs. C. G. Gasqu event of the afternoon was match between an Authe captained by Mr. J. B. and an Actresses' XI, capt Miss Gladys Cooper, w

H.R.H. Princess Alice and Fr. Jellicoe at the Garden Fête at "The Elms," Hampstead

Authors proved triumphant. This was followed by an address on housing by Priestley, and an auction of a canvas on which Mr. Philip de Laszlo was to portrait sketch. The Princess made a tour of the grounds, and was much interest stalls and in the model of the overcrowded room also on view.

During both the afternoon and the evening, scenes from "The People's Pagea Pancras" were given. Side shows provided all kinds of amusement, and the final a symbolic burning of the overcrowded room by Mr. H. R. Selley, M.P., Chairm L.C.C. Housing Committee.

Results from the Garden Party have been splendid, and, in addition to donation £350, over £400 of shares, etc., have been taken up.

An excerpt from Housing happenings showing a photo of Basil Jellicoe with a model 'slum room' on tour to show the conditions of the poor in order to prompt investment. It makes clear the connections of aristocracy and literary circles to the cause.

SOCIAL HOUSING

BEFORE SOCIAL HOUSING

BY DEBORAH LAVIN

Social Housing existed before Social Housing, it was just called something else; and it goes without saying that there was never enough of it.

No one knows when the first almshouses for the "halt, the lame and the blind" or the aged poor were established, but St. Oswald's Almshouses, which still function at Upper Tything, Worcester, are supposed to have been founded about the year 990, though no documentation survives before the mid-13th century. The Hospital of St. Cross and Almshouses of Noble Poverty at Winchester was founded in 1132, by a grandson of William the Conqueror.

These are just the tip of an almshouse iceberg. Usually set up by individual philanthropic endowment, they were invariably attached to a church or religious order. Many were disbanded at the Reformation, which decimated the medieval welfare system, yet it was not long before new almshouses were established by philanthropic Anglicans.

There were conditions for entry, applicants not only had to fulfil the criteria of being 'halt, blind or lame' or being aged poor, but they had to be of good standing in the community and a regular church attender.

As there were invariably more applicants than places, there was a social control element inherent in the admissions procedure. Anyone anticipating they might need to apply for an almshouse later on in life would adapt their behaviour accordingly.

Almshouses were never intended for the able-bodied unemployed or widows (or other unsupported women with children), as their problems were essentially seen as temporary, and except for widows, they were also seen to some degree as self-inflicted.

Even so, the Elizabethan Poor Laws passed in 1599 and 1601 instigated a local rate (tax) to help the temporary poor with rent, food and fuel costs. These new Poor Laws also helped any disabled or old people who had not found a place in the more generous almshouses system, sometimes by helping them in their own homes, sometimes by gathering them together in "poorhouses", which were less generous than almshouses but not as punitive as workhouses. These were set up later, at a time when the government took on a harsher attitude to the poor.

The Elizabethan Poor Law prevailed until the 1834 Poor Law Amendment Act took a wrecking ball to it. Sometimes it was operated harshly, sometimes surprisingly generously, but behind it was:

THE CONCEPT THAT EVERYONE BORN HAD THE RIGHT TO MAINTENANCE.

It was an idea in direct conflict with the aggressive capitalism which developed in the late 18th century and early 19th century, when men such as Jeremy Bentham and Thomas Malthus began to argue that no one had any right to live, if they could not maintain themselves.

This brutal thinking informed the 1834 Poor Law Amendment Act, which abolished all help for the poor, unless they entered one of the newly-built workhouses that began to pepper the country.

In the workhouse, unless they were too old to have further children, husbands and wives were separated from each other and with the exception of nursing babes in arms, mothers were separated from their children.

Any disabled or aged poor not lucky enough to have an almshouse place would also be refused any help outside the prison-like workhouse, where everyone wore workhouse garb, ate cheap, non-nutritious food and worked all day picking oakum or doing something equally hard and unpleasant.

In Oliver Twist, published just a year after the new workhouse system was introduced, Charles

News piece about the Peabody dwellings.

The St. Pancras Hospital, the old workhouse.

Dickens described the grim life of this new workhouse system for children, but though the book was a best seller, the bad publicity brought no immediate changes to the new workhouse system, as in the eyes of the Whig (Liberal) government, it was effective in making just about any job at any low rate of pay more attractive than being dependent on the poor law.

And it was certainly true as any man living in the country or some small town, who found himself unemployed:

...WOULD RATHER TRUDGE (WITH THEIR FAMILIES) TO THE CITIES OF THE INDUSTRIAL NORTH OR TO LONDON, WHERE THERE WAS ALWAYS LOW PAID WORK AND TERRIBLE HOUSING. THIS WAS AT LEAST WAS BETTER THAN THE WORKHOUSE.

The disabled and aged poor could not trudge to the cities in search of work, and if they could not find a place in an almshouse, they were forced into the prison of the workhouse.

In the early days of the new workhouse system, the Victorians might be able to accept the "feckless" unemployed being sent to the workhouse, but many were horrified at the idea of the aged poor who had worked all their lives, or the disabled, enduring what amounted to prison. Ironically, the harsh new 1834 Poor Law heralded in a flurry of new foundations of almshouses, not just in the country, but in the cities.

In 1860, St. Pancras Church opened the doors of a hundred new almshouses places, which they described as providing for:

'THOSE DECAYED, BUT RESPECTABLE PARISHIONERS WHO, AT THE CLOSE OF LIVES SPENT IN ARDUOUS BUT UNSUCCESSFUL STRUGGLES FOR MAINTENANCE, FIND THEMSELVES REDUCED TO THE ALTERNATIVE OF SINKING WANT OR PRIVATION OR OF ACCEPTING THE PAINFUL AND HUMILIATING POSITION OF INMATES OF THE WORKHOUSE.'

At St. Pancras, elderly husbands and wives were allowed to stay together and the poorest were given a weekly maintenance grant (pension).

St. Pancras was one of many such church-based philanthropic schemes, not only in Camden but up and down the country, but such schemes did not meet the need either for the disabled or aged poor and did nothing to help the terrible housing conditions of the working poor.

The problem also caught the eye of the millionaire George Peabody, who stepped in to provide housing for working class families. And having inherited a small sum, so did John Ruskin, who got Octavia Hill interested in a small working class housing project in Marylebone, before she branched out on her own into bigger projects.

Other philanthropists followed, including those of the Guinness Trust in the 1890s, along with all kinds of other smaller schemes for 'working class dwellings'.

One problem was shared by all these projects. They only took the better-off working class as tenants, as no slack was given with rent arrears; and any family who could not pay the rent was evicted. And with a Poor Law still generally only offering the "help of the workhouse", only the better-off working class could afford membership of a Friendly Society to help them over slack times.

By the end of the 19th century, even the most obtuse could see neither philanthropy or traditional almshouse schemes were ever going to provide decent housing to lower-paid working-class families at an affordable price.

It would have to be provided by the municipality. In London that meant either the local borough council or the London Country Council (set up in 1888). It was also beginning to be understood that tolerating some rent arrears might better than breaking up a home and sending an entire family to the workhouse, but that and the rest of the intertwined story of housing and welfare is told elsewhere.

What matters here is that the existence of social housing before social housing, like the existence of a Poor Law from 1601, is a significant part of cultural history.

It is indeed more important to narrate than the 1834 Poor Law Amendment Act and the many other schemes intermittently introduced to punish the poor for their poverty.

DEBORAH LAVIN IS A SOCIAL HISTORIAN AND LIVED IN COOPERS LANE, SOMERS TOWN

I am not a historian of housing and the focus of this little article is going to be an overview of Fr Basil's life and motivation – but with a particular emphasis, of course, on his lasting achievements in terms of the provision of social housing, which still provides his triumphant legacy in Somers Town.

It should be said at the outset that there were, of course, clergymen – and lay people - of all denominations working to alleviate the conditions of the London poor.

Nonetheless, there is no doubt that the High Church Anglo-Catholic Movement seemed to have provided a particular motivation to many notable individuals to give their lives to the people of the slums.

It was estimated by the commission that:

THE WORK OF THE MIDLAND RAILWAY LED TO THE LOSS OF ABOUT FIVE HUNDRED HOUSES IN SOMERS TOWN, AND THE DECANTING OF ALMOST SIX THOUSAND INHABITANTS INTO THE SURROUNDING DISTRICTS.

The commission expressed the opinion that one reason that the houses of the poor were most frequently chosen for demolition (which caused the greatest human misery) was that they were the cheapest to purchase. Permissive legislation did permit the demolition of slums and the building of houses, but there was often an unwillingness to carry out such measures due to the expense and the predominance of property owners on representative bodies.

HERO OF TEN THOUSAND HOMES

FR JELLICOE'S HOUSING SCHEME IN SOMERS TOWN

BY PAUL SHAW

One of Fr Basil's own greatest models and heroes was Fr Arthur Henry Stanton, curate at one of the most famous 'ritualist' churches, nearby in the current borough of Camden, St. Alban's Holborn. These Anglo-Catholic 'slum priests' were even immortalised in popular fiction.

Many, like Fr Basil himself, came from privileged backgrounds – and it should not be forgotten that the Anglican Church also provided a place for women to serve the poor of the slums, so long as they were willing to take religious vows, in the revived Anglican Sisterhoods.

Fr Basil's special achievement was to galvanise and inspire rich and poor alike to improve the lives of the slum dwellers of Somers Town, and, within the space of his short life, establish a practical scheme by which the slums of the area could be swept away and replaced with high quality housing.

But it is important also to recognise that his intention – and his vision – was not only to build homes, but to build communities: as he famously said 'housing is not enough',

The problems he addressed in the Somers Town slums are described by the evidence and reports presented to the Royal Commission on the Housing of the Working Classes, of 1884-5.

Housing reformers such as Octavia Hill had brought forward voluntary schemes for the building of artisans' dwellings, and certainly provided a precedent for the work of Fr Basil, but such schemes seldom addressed the needs of the poorest slum dwellers. By 1912-13, house building was stagnating in central London, and the housing which was being built was largely for members of the artisanal class, with little for the poorest, who could only afford to rent two or three rooms, whatever the size of their families. St. Pancras Borough Council made very slow progress, leaving others to take the lead, and by 1912 building of new homes was failing to keep up with demolition of the slums.

Long before Fr Basil came along, the church with which he was most closely associated, St. Mary's in Eversholt Street, was involved in the amelioration of the lives of the poor.

The church may be seen as a good example of the response of the Church of England to the growth of urban populations, and to the needs of the poor; and additionally to the increasing and often controversial influence of the Anglo-Catholic movement within the Church.

A charming though rather ungainly early example of the Gothic Revival, St. Mary's was built 1822-4, and consecrated in May 1826, originally as a district chapel of St. Pancras Church. It was often referred to as the 'cabbies' church' due to its mission to cab drivers using the old Euston Station.

By the late nineteenth century, the church had thrown in its lot with the increasingly influential Anglo-Catholic Movement. A vicar of the church at this period, Rev W A Beaumont, said on one occasion of his parish that there is

'NO MORE POVERTY STRICKEN DISTRICT IN LONDON' WHERE THE RESIDENTS OF HIS PARISH WERE 'PACKED TOGETHER MORE CLOSELY PERHAPS THAN IN EAST LONDON'.

He complained that the railway companies, who had caused much of the overcrowding, contributed nothing corporately to the upkeep of the poor. However, he showed great pride in the great panoply of clubs and social organisations established by the parish to serve the needs of the populace.

Fortunately, the needs of the poor of Somers Town was recognised by one section of the establishment: Magdalen College Oxford. From 1908 its Anglican Mission was based in Somers Town, following its founding in 1884 and previous moves to Stepney, Shoreditch and Portsea. The Oxford Colleges had been reforming themselves in the the nineteenth century, and the nurturing of a sense of social responsibility came to be essential to the life of the students.

The move to Somers Town took place to make the mission more accessible to undergraduates. The years from 1908 to 1914 saw the establishment of new parish clubs for both sexes, and the active involvement of undergraduates and old members of the college in the parish of St. Mary's. From 1909 to 1911 as many as seventeen Magdalen members helped regularly with the clubs and eighty-five college members, including Edward, Prince of Wales, visited the mission. In 1922 Fr Basil Jellicoe was appointed Magdalen Missioner, and a new and energising force was now to enter the parish

John Basil Lee Jellicoe was born on February 5th 1899, in Chailey, Sussex, eight miles from Lewes. His father was rector of the parish, and his vocation for the priesthood seems to have been present from Basil's earliest years. Early on, he was said to evince both a consciousness of the evils of poverty, and a contempt for class boundaries.

He was educated first in Brighton, a great centre of Anglo-Catholicism, then at the public school Haileybury, leaving in 1915. An early oration to a gathering from the friendly society the Oddfellows was on the subject of Christian Socialism, and was counted a success.

HE WAS A DAB HAND WITH THE ACCORDION, TO WHICH HE COULD SING COMIC SONGS, AN EARLY EXAMPLE OF HIS 'COMMON TOUCH'.

He went to Magdalen in 1917, but the following year he entered the navy. This service was in a way most appropriate, as his uncle was Admiral Lord Jellicoe! He served on the warship Iron Duke, actually seeing service against the Soviet government in the bombardment of Sebastopol, during the futile Allied campaign in support of the White Russian forces.

He was demobilized in 1920. From the first, his Christian faith seems to have been a highly practical rather than a theoretical or intellectual one, and Fr Geoffrey Studdert Kennedy (the famous 'Woodbine Willie') and Fr Stanton were said to be those Anglican clergymen whom he most admired. As a young seminarian, he so impressed the Bishop of London that he was released from his clerical training at St. Stephen's House a year early to become missioner in Somers Town.

When Fr Basil arrived at the mission, there were severe problems, notably due to wartime -debt, and the effective division of work of the mission from that of the parish.

He threw himself into the work of the boys' and girls' clubs, and added others for example a troop of scouts, a boxing club, and a nursery school. He had a boyish charm, a great sense of fun, and an extreme empathy for his parishioners, which they sensed;

CHILDREN LOVED HIM AND CHASED AND CLAMOURED AFTER HIM AS HE WALKED THE STREETS.

He was apparently not an eloquent preacher: he was persuasive because of the simplicity, conviction and passion with which he gave voice to his vision. Gradually, he built up a clergy team. From March 1922 he was assisted by Fr Percy Maryon-Wilson as Assistant Missioner, who in 1929 became vicar of the parish. Another new curate in 1919 was Fr Desmond Morse-Boycott, a voracious writer in support of Anglo-Catholic causes, who dedicated himself to providing education for poor boys in the parish, and who trained the boys for the church choir.

The Prince of Wales first visited in December 1923, and he agreed to be patron of the Mission. Even at this early stage, there was concern over Fr Basil's overworking. Fits of energy were followed by depression, and he had even considered resignation, abandoned only when he realised that this might actually mean the end of the Magdalen Mission. There are descriptions of him bursting into his friend's room in the early hours of the morning crying out:

'I SHALL HAVE TO RESIGN AFTER ALL. I KNOW I SHALL HAVE TO RESIGN. I'M GOING TO RESIGN NOW'.

And his friend would reasonably reply: 'But, my dear Basil, you can't possibly resign at three o'clock in the morning'. Fr Basil was by temperament a sensitive individual.

Stories differ as to what first moved Fr Basil to take up the issue of housing as his first priority, but there was clearly a realisation very early on that unless the slums were dealt with, any other forms of social amelioration could only be regarded as tinkering with the problem.

Fr Morse-Boycott cites an incident where he found a live rat under a sick boy's pillow as being the moment of decision. To Fr Basil, that such conditions could exist after the so-called 'Great War' for civilisation was an affront to humanity. Of the condition of the slum houses themselves, they were often originally quite decent, large and substantial buildings, intended for lower-middle class families with servants, but chronic overcrowding, neglect, and infestation with bugs and vermin had left most in a terrible state. It has been estimated that 22,000 lived in the parish, with an average occupancy of two to three per room.

Fr Basil wrote in December 1925:

'HOSPITALS, CLINICS, DAY NURSERIES, SCOUTS' CAMPS, OUTINGS AND ALL THE SPLENDID WORK WHICH IS BEING CARRIED ON...[IS] PRACTICALLY WASTED ON THOSE WHO HAVE TO BE SENT BACK TO LIVE SEVEN OR EIGHT IN ONE ROOM WITHOUT PROPER AIR OR LIGHT, OR THE MERE DECENCIES OF LIFE.'

'He spoke of the people of Somers Town as "blood relations of the King of Kings" and stressed the infinite dignity of human nature as ennobled by the Incarnation of the Son of God.' [1]

The poor were not seen primarily as sinners, or as those who were lacking in the moral fibre or spiritual strength to improve themselves, but as the class of people with whom Christ had chosen to spend his time on earth. Fr Basil once said:

'THE WORK WE ARE DOING IN SOMERS TOWN...AND ALL SOCIAL SERVICES WORK, BEGAN IN A MANGER. ONE OF THE WORST TRAGEDIES OF THE SLUMS IS THE OVER-CROWDING. OUR LORD CAME DOWN TO FACE THE VERY CONDITIONS WHICH WE ARE FACING TODAY IN THE LONDON SLUMS.'

Father Basil Jellicoe in Somers Town with a crowd. Photo St. Pancras Housing Collection, courtesy of the Camden Local Studies and Archives Centre.

The practical beginning of the housing scheme came about when it was realised that there were a number of derelict houses in the parish standing empty. It proved very difficult even to identify the landlords, whom Fr Basil observed were often happy to allow properties to empty and fall into decay in the hope that they could later be sold at a profit. In July 1924 a limited liability company was formed, with the aim of:

'...ACQUIRING HOUSES, WHICH BY MEANS OF SCIENTIFIC MANAGEMENT & SUCH STRUCTURAL ALTERATIONS AS MAY BE NECESSARY SHALL BE CONVERTED INTO IMPROVED... WORKING CLASS DWELLINGS'.

At the meeting were Fr Basil in the chair, Fr Percy Maryon-Wilson and Leonard Atkinson from the Magdalen College Mission; Miss Edith Neville, Secretary of St.

Pancras Council of Social Service; and various others with the requisite professional skill and knowledge.

The first aim was to purchase the freeholds of eight houses in Gee Street and Clarendon Street, at a cost of £3,000. An appeal was successful in bringing in around £8,000 in the space of five months. Large donations came in from society figures, financial institutions and Anglo-Catholic congregations.

Those cynics who said that slum dwellers were too irresponsible to pay their rents on time were proved wrong. Fr Basil emphasised that the success of the housing project was greatly due to the trustful relationship which had grown up between the staff at St. Mary's and their poor parishioners.

But he was also able to use his privileged background to obtain the support of individuals such as the Archbishop of Canterbury, the Prince of Wales, the Minister of Housing, and of course, his own uncle, Earl Jellicoe of Scarpa. Jellicoe demonstrated an uncanny ability to inveigle the contemporary media – films, the press, and the lecture circuit – into spreading his message.

Often, over 130 talks would be given in a year, by Fr Basil or his fellow priests. Over 10,000 copies of the periodical Housing Happenings were distributed to supporters in the 1930s: he not only edited the journal in its early years, but appears to have written a great deal of it himself.

One particular concern was that the new housing should be affordable by the poor, and that poor communities should not be broken up. In 1928, in the first issue of Housing Happenings, Fr Basil wrote:

'WE WANT IT TO BE UNDERSTOOD THAT THE VAST MAJORITY OF OUR TENANTS MUST LIVE IN THE DISTRICT, AND CANNOT AFFORD TO MOVE TO THE VARIOUS HOUSING ESTATES OUTSIDE LONDON WITHOUT LOSS OF WORK AND EXPENDITURE IN TRAVELLING.'

By 1933, six acres of land had been acquired in the Somers Town area, and the society had erected buildings containing 170 flats. The houses purchased by the society proved to be in such a deplorable condition, that the preferred solution was to demolish them and start from scratch.

The culmination of the early history of the society, the

1   Biographer Kenneth Ingram

Sidney Estate, was opened on a two-and-half acre site in May 1938, and provided housing for around 1,000 persons in modern flats. Better housing was only the first step to establishing integrated and well-served communities. This led, among other things, to the establishment of a loan club, a furnishing company and a children's holiday club.

Father Jellicoe in the Anchor pub in Somers Town singing with a crowd. Still taken from an archival film that can be seen at spirit.aspaceforus.club

One of the major concerns of Irene Barclay and others involved in the early history of the housing association was to ensure that the housing was not only functional, that there was a spirit of beauty, charm and grace animating the developments. To this end, in the early schemes the artist Gilbert Bayes was commissioned to provide beautiful ceramic decorative features to grace the dignified and expansive ranges of flats. To the outrage of the temperance lobby, Fr Basil also said:

'I AM LONGING FOR THE TIME WHEN I CAN RUN A "PUB"...'

and eventually the society took over the Anchor and Tavistock Arms public houses. Ultimately, this scheme did not last, but the aim was the laudable one of creating family-friendly establishments which would be asserts to the community rather than disfiguring centres of drunkenness and immorality. Fr Basil even expressed the desire to establish a Christian night club!

Tragically, he did not even live to see the opening of the Sidney Estate. He had had a number of breakdowns, and in 1933, the committee of the housing association felt they had no option but to ask him to resign as chairman and organiser and accept the paid position of 'founder'.

Fr Basil was so upset by this request, that he resigned in 1934, rarely visiting Somers Town thereafter. He found a base for a time at St. Martin's-in-the-Fields, where he could celebrate the Eucharist daily.

A story is that some of his friends questioned how he could work in a church so 'low' in its churchmanship that they did not even have Reservation of the Blessed Sacrament, but Fr Basil's characteristic reply was that they did reserve the homeless in the crypt. Very unwisely for his health, he continued his propagandistic work in support of housing reform elsewhere.

By June 1935, it seemed as if his overworked frame could take no more, and he had another another collapse; he was unable to fight off pneumonia in his weakened state, and he died only aged only thirty-six on 23rd August, in a nursing home in Uxbridge.

As he lapsed into a final coma, the nurses saw him raising his hands and murmuring in what appeared to be a foreign language: it is said that he was saying the Latin Mass, which he knew by heart.

A particularly moving recollection was left by Rev W H Elliott, who knew Fr Basil only in the last few months of his life:

'I CAN SEE HIM NOW, PACING UP AND DOWN THE CARPET AND ROUND AND ROUND THE ROOM, A SOUL ON FIRE WITHIN A RATHER FADED CASSOCK, HIS EYES ABLAZE WITH WHAT I CAN ONLY CALL A FURY OF FAITH FOR THE RIGHTING OF ANCIENT WRONGS, HIS HEART AGLOW WITH AFFECTION FOR ALL SORTS AND CONDITIONS OF MEN AND WITH VISIONS OF THEIR GREATER GOOD. I WONDERED HOW LONG IT WOULD TAKE FOR SO KEEN A FLAME TO BURN HIM OUT. SO WHEN ON A DARK DAY IN AUGUST THE NEWS OF HIS DEATH CAME TO ME ... I FELT AT ONCE, AS I FEEL NOW, THAT IF EVER A MAN IN OUR TIME WAS CARRIED BY THE FIRE OF HIS OWN PERSONALITY INTO THE HEAVENLY PLACES THAT MAN WAS BASIL JELLICOE...'

But he might have been most touched by the tribute in his obituary in the Church Times, (from which the title of this article has been borrowed) penned by his priestly colleague, Fr Morse-Boycott:

'THE CHURCH MOURNS THE LOSS OF ONE OF HER DEVOTED SONS, WHO HAS WRITTEN A TRACT FOR THE TIMES IN STONE, A SIGN TO THOSE WHO COME THAT WITH GOD'S HELP ALL IS POSSIBLE.'

PAUL SHAW IS A HISTORIAN

© Copyright 2019

'Art in Everyday life' work comissioned by the St. Pancras Housing Improvement Society: Gilbert Bayes' Finials from poem '24 Tailors and a Snail', on top of drying posts in flats in Somers Town , now sadly missing. Photo St. Pancras Housing Improvement Society. Courtesy of the Camden Local Studies and Archives Centre.

IRENE BARCLAY

SOMERS TOWN SURVEYOR

BY CARRIE DE SILVA

Irene Barclay was the first woman to qualify as a chartered surveyor, in the Valuation Division in 1922.

Born Irene Turberville Martin into a socialist family in Hereford in 1894, her father, Basil, was a non-conformist minister whose memoirs, An Impossible Parson, set out the philosophy of public service, faith and wry sense of fun which informed her upbringing. Barclay was the eldest of four. Her brother, Kingsley, was an occasional lecturer in politics at the LSE, a committed pacifist, and editor of The New Statesman from 1930-60.

Barclay attended Hereford High School, which she loved, until 1911. She then boarded at Monmouth High for two years, where she was 'miserable in the extreme'. Having grown up in reasonable comfort, in 1913 the family moved to Finchley in somewhat straightened circumstances. Barclay gained a BA (Hons) in History in 1916 followed by a diploma in Social Science in 1917, both from Bedford College.

Work experience during Barclay's Social Science diploma introduced her to London's slums and to Miss Maud Jeffery, formerly secretary to Octavia Hill and now a housing manager for the Crown Estate Commissioners. Miss Jeffery ensured that Barclay became an early member of the Association of Women House Property Managers and encouraged her to study for surveying exams.

So Barclay took evening classes in surveying alongside Evelyn Perry, the second woman to be admitted, and they referred, with ill-concealed mischief, to tutors' embarrassment at having women present in lectures on drainage and sanitation. She was employed throughout her training period by the Crown Office on a salary which reached £140 per year by the time she left - 'stingy' (in Barclay's word) even by contemporary measures.

On qualifying, Barclay spent six months with Louis de Soissons, architect of the new Welwyn Garden City, but she soon set up in on her own account in Finsbury Square.

She ran the practice, largely in partnership with Evelyn Perry, in Somers Town (the area around St. Pancras, King's Cross and Euston stations), for over 50 years.

BARCLAY'S WORKING LIFE WAS SPENT IMPROVING LONDON SOCIAL HOUSING AND SHE WAS INVOLVED FROM THE EARLIEST DAYS WITH THE ST. PANCRAS HOUSING ASSOCIATION BECOMING SECRETARY OF THE SOCIETY IN 1925, HOLDING THE OFFICE FOR 48 YEARS.

The Society's first project was to purchase and refurbish seven houses. Barclay later favoured demolition and re-development over refurbishment once the extent of damp, dry rot, poor structure and, not least, bed bug infestation, became apparent.

A key feature of housing association developments managed by Barclay and Perry, distinguishing them from council programmes, was re-housing within communities, to retain community bonds, an ethos reflected in the title of her 1976 record of working and, to some extent, personal life, People Need Roots.

Barclay and her partners also achieved some of their success through shrewd financial management, for example running an in-house workforce for general maintenance, only sub-contracting large structural programmes, even then ensuring that all materials were purchased direct.

Barclay was active in fundraising and notes giving many talks where she bridled at and countered perceptions of the slum population, which attitudes she described as 'a libellous insult to the mass of poorer working-class people'.

Along with the St. Pancras work, Barclay's firm took on the establishment and management of other housing associations, council estate management, private professional work and some voluntary activities.

She also supported tenants in their struggles with landlords and loan sharks, which led to a loan club and furniture shop. In addition, Barclay worked to provide accommodation for the elderly, nurseries, play areas, seaside holidays and a children's home in the country, her deep compassion and politics always manifest in practical measures.

In the decades of mass slum clearance, Barclay and Perry broke new ground with their surveys, commissioned both privately and by local authorities, which were unique in the extent of internal surveying and engagement with residents, as opposed to the more cursory, external surveys more usually produced by councils. This not only gained tenants' support but provided depth to discussions of housing need.

Barclay was a prolific speaker, broadcaster and writer, often for the left-leaning press. And writing and speaking invitations increased considerably on the publication of the influential war-time report, Our Towns: a Close-up, produced in 1943 by the Women's Group on Public Welfare (of which she was a member) at the request of the National Federation of Women's Institutes when evacuation disclosed the hygiene, nutrition and behavioural standards of small proportion of evacuees to be of concern. She also edited the annual property journal House Happenings for some time after the war.

Barclay expressed a lack of time in her early career and war years to keep up with professional groups: the Soroptomists, the Society of Women Housing Managers (SWHM) and, of course the Surveyors' Institution.

At the end of the war, however, she became chairman of the SWHM and drove the dropping of the 'W' and the introduction of men. After the war Barclay continued to campaign for better housing and joined a number of public committees and boards, expressing the hope that she was chosen as a surveyor and not as a token women!

Unlike many career women in the first half of the twentieth century, Barclay married and had two sons, Michael and Anthony.

In 1966 Barclay was widowed and received on OBE for her work with housing associations. She retired in 1972 and died in Toronto in 1989, having moved to Canada a few years earlier to be near her younger son.

In a letter of 7th September 1925 to her old university tutor Barclay expressed sorrow:

'IF NO MORE WOMEN SURVEYORS FOLLOW ON, AS IT REALLY IS A JOB IN WHICH A WOMAN MAY BE VERY USEFUL'.

In the following decades even in her own business she voiced disappointment that, despite training many women housing managers, relatively few went on to qualify as surveyors. Still she would, I venture, be shocked that in 2017, 86 out of every 100 chartered surveyors are men.

CARRIE DE SLIVA IS A PRINCIPAL LECTURER IN LAW AND TAXATION, HARPER ADAMS UNIVERSITY

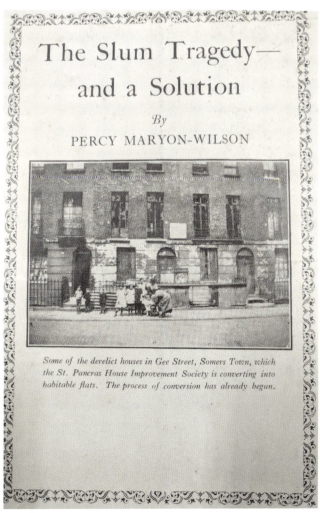

The Slum Tragedy—
and a Solution

By
PERCY MARYON-WILSON

Some of the derelict houses in Gee Street, Somers Town, which the St. Pancras House Improvement Society is converting into habitable flats. The process of conversion has already begun.

JOYCE, ST. FRANCIS' FLATS WITH HER GRANDAUGHTER

"I look after her for her once a week for her mum who works. I've lived in Somers Town all my life. When I was a child, I went on all the trips they organised - my mum was 'Fat Flo' she took all the kids to Wales with the clubs. She was a character - took part in the pantomine - the mum's club. She played Friar Tuck. They'd all come home and be singing. Her picture's on the wall here.
I'm so cross about the Bayes finials going missing - they were taken. They were meant for us."

Photo by John Carroll

PAUL, ARTIST, RETIRED, ST. AUGUSTINE'S HOUSE

"My family have been in Somers Town for generations. My nan was an unofficial midwife - there was no NHS then so the women helped each other out. She'd be called out in the middle of the night.
I went to university, then came back here. I worked in the library archives, and set up a community garden back in the 1970s. The painting behind me I did recently - art is my life now. I'm busy doing printmaking and I'm in a choir."

Photo by John Carroll

JOHN, EX-BOXING TRAINER, ST. MARGARET'S HOUSING

"My family have been in Somers Town for years. I grew up in St. Mary's Flats in 1969. My dad, Peter, was a boxing trainer, and ran a boxing club in Covent Garden. I followed him and trained - I was pretty handy myself - a bantamweight as a youth. My proudest moment was training John Mugabi, a middleweight champion, from Uganda. We had a gym at the German Gymnasium - it's a fancy restaurant now.
The area's changed - someone said the name will go and it'll become 'East Euston Quarter' but the warmth is stiil in the community in Somers Town."

Photo by Diana Foster

BUILDING

"the council believed that with perseverance and courage, it would achieve something in giving the poor people in Somers Town the first real chance they ever had. Borough councils had built housing for the respectable, they atttracted the nice people, and the people for whom the houses were intended never got there; but in this instance those who lived in the old houses were now living in the new - a genuine transition."

- AJ Thomas, Architect of the Aldenham and Wolcot House scheme, 1928

St. Pancras Housing Society Rent book, kindly donated by George Sharp.

PEOPLE NEED ROOTS

BY ALAN STEPHENS

I moved to the Drummond Estate as a teenager in the early 1960s and lived there until the early 1990s. During that period I witnessed (along with my neighbours and friends) all the changes that occurred in those years, such as the refurbishment and modernisation of the flats and the decanting of many families during the process. There was always

Alan (though not a royalist) at the 1977 Jubilee Street Party held in the courtyards of St. Pancras Housing flats.
Photo courtesy of Alan Stephens,

a close-knit community on the estate. I remember the bunting and decorations that were put up during the Queen's Silver Jubilee in 1977; and the children's party (if my memory serves me correctly) organised to commemorate VE day 1945 in 1985.

The St. Pancras Housing Association always truly reflected the ethos and values that inspired the founders during those years in terms of the Tenant/Landlord relationship. The cohesiveness of the local community on the estate was a defining characteristic of the period. Sadly, however, with the loss of so many local pubs in the Somers Town area, that aspect of community life is now much diminished, although it may still flourish, to a certain extent, in the local cafes. Café culture? Maybe.

With the arrival of HS2, unless, we hope, it is cancelled, and with the possibility of Crossrail 2 and the proposed redevelopment of Euston station, wholesale upheaval and disruption is threatened in the Somers Town area in the near future. It is important that the past memories of local people are 'captured' for posterity.

ALAN STEPHENS IS RETIRED, REPRESENTS TENANTS ON HIS TRA, AND LIVES IN ST. PANCRAS HOUSING
'People need roots' is the title of a book by Irene Barclay.

Record of inhabitants of Levita House on the eve of the war.

A BRIEF GUIDE

TO HOUSING ACTS AND SOMERS TOWN

BY JACKIE LEWIS AND MICHAEL PARKES

'I TAKE IT AS A STARTING POINT THAT IT IS NOT THE DUTY OF THE GOVERNMENT TO PROVIDE ANY CLASS OF CITIZENS WITH ANY OF THE NECESSARIES OF LIFE, AND AMONG THE NECESSARIES OF LIFE WE MUST OF COURSE INCLUDE GOOD AND HABITABLE DWELLINGS. IF IT DID SO, IT WOULD INEVITABLY TEND TO MAKE THAT CLASS DEPEND, NOT ON THEMSELVES, BUT UPON WHAT WAS DONE FOR THEM ELSEWHERE'

Sir Richard Cross Home Secretary 1874-1880 1885-1886 – British Statesman and Conservative Politician

For most of the 19th and early part of the 20th century the majority of working class people in cities were forced to live in appalling conditions. Despite concerns from public health reformers, writers and progressive politicians, and the sensationalist descriptions of the vice and moral decay in the 'slums', national legislation and central government subsidy for housing reform was not considered a priority or obligation.

By the end of the 19th century, there was an acknowledgement that the provision of affordable sanitary housing could not just be left to the private market or philanthropic organisations. The London County Council was formed in 1889 and with the full sanction of the 1890 Housing of the Working Classes Act began a progressive and innovative slum clearance and house building programme.

BACKGROUND TO SOMERS TOWN SLUMS

Somers Town originally in the medieval Parish of St. Pancras , Middlesex, in 1900 became the Metropolitan Borough of St. Pancras.

In 1784, the Polygon (a 15-sided block comprising 32 houses) was built amid fields, brick works, dust heaps, and market gardens. The area was initially fashionable and appears to have appealed to middle-class people fleeing the French Revolution. The Polygon deteriorated socially as the surrounding land was subsequently sold off in smaller lots for cheaper housing, especially after the start of construction in the 1830's of the railway lines into Euston, St Pancras and King's Cross.

In this period the area housed a large transient population of labourers and the population density of the area soared. By the late 19th century most of the houses were in multiple occupation, and overcrowding was severe with whole families sometimes living in one room, as recorded in the social surveys of Charles Booth and Irene Barclay.

HOUSING ACTS

1875 – ARTISANS AND LABOURERS DWELLINGS IMPROVEMENT ACT

Designed to permit local authorities to purchase and clear areas of unfit dwellings and rehouse those displaced. Local authority could provide the rehousing but without subsidy from rates or government.

1890 – HOUSING OF THE WORKING CLASSES ACT

This basically ushers in local authority housing in London. For the first time, certain local authorities could build housing to add to their stock.

It gave local authorities powers to acquire land by compulsory purchase order.

This was Important in that it gave councils the power not just to clear slum areas, but also to build municipal housing for displaced residents.

The LCC made full use of the Act.

1898 – LONDON COUNTY COUNCIL COMES INTO BEING

The formation of the LCC brings in significant changes to the perception of local government. The Progressive group on the Council, who formed the majority until 1907, were drawn from Fabian Socialists (Tony Benn's grandfather John was one), liberals and labour leaders. They established an Architects Department in 1893 dedicated to the Housing of the Working Classes.

The LCC architects were also committed to building working-class housing with an eye to aesthetics and style, a reaction to the stark uniformity of the 'model dwellings' of the Peabody Trust.

Much in the same way, the visionary architect Sydney Cook of Camden Council's Architects Department reacted against the uniformity and starkness of the standard high-rise builds of the 1960s.

They employed young talented architects like Owen Fleming, who combined their socialist beliefs and their architectural skills into their planning and designs.

They were heavily influenced by John Ruskin and the Arts and Crafts Movements, which can be clearly seen in their surviving buildings.

THE THREE MAJOR AND HIGHLY INNOVATIVE 'TENEMENT' ESTATES LCC BETWEEN 1901 – 1909

These were Millbank Estate (Westminster) , Boundary Estate (Shoreditch) - designed by Owen Fleming, and considered to be the world's first 'council estate' and the Bourne Estate (Holborn), which was much admired and copied as an example of high-standard public housing.

None of the new tenements shared toilets or kitchens and most were self-contained with spacious courtyards and landscaping.

There were concerns by detractors that the provision of this standard of housing would 'sap' the spirit of the lower classes and make life too comfortable for them to improve their lot.

This theme is echoed time and time again down the decades – Neave Brown recalled that when shown the interiors of the flats in Alexandra Road a councillor commented in much the same way about the indulgence

of giving council tenants Habitat-style quality interiors.

Unfortunately, the higher rents demanded by these new builds failed to help the people it intended to help the most. The very poorest could not afford the rents so the new homes appealed mainly to the better off working classes in skilled and steady employment.

The hope was that when the better off moved into these new builds the poorest could then move into their vacated properties.

1900 – HOUSING OF THE WORKING CLASSES ACT AND THE CREATION OF METROPOLITAN BOROUGHS

Metropolitan Boroughs become the principal providers of housing in inner London, but only 11 of the 28 new borough councils built anything between 1890-1913.

London County Council (LCC) Churchway Scheme: Wellesley, Somerset and Seymour Buildings Built 1901 - 1910

The LCC was formed in 1889. It was the first London-wide general municipal authority to be directly elected and was replaced in 1965 by the Greater London Council. The impetus for slum clearance before WW1 came with Part 1 of the Housing of the Working Classes Act 1890.

The decision to redevelop rested in part on relative death rate for the area (St. Pancras 20.1 per thousand. Churchway 33.1 per thousand).

LCC Architects design was influenced by the Arts and Crafts. The Buildings are of solid construction, with Somerset and Seymour having more character and style than the slightly earlier Wellesley Buildings. A store next to Somerset Buildings had a Temperance Bar, which fits in well with Lady Somerset owning the land, who was convinced, like many prominent Victorians, that drink was at the root of most poverty.

St. Pancras Borough Council leads the way. In 1909 St. Pancras opened a small block of tenements in Flaxman Terrace. It was one of the few boroughs building anything.

There was still no government subsidy except in the form of favourable borrowing rates. Housing schemes couldn't be subsidised from the rates so rent levels would be impossibly high. As a result, little building took place.

Amendments then allowed local authorities to build outside their own area. The LCC concentrated on building cottage estates in 'suburbs' like Tooting's Totterdown Fields Estate inspired by The Garden Cities Association formed in 1898.

The 'garden suburb' movement intended building economically self-sufficient and socially-mixed new towns, charging lower rents for the working classes. Hampstead Garden Suburb, built in 1906, was intended as such a community.

However, the quality of the building and the rents that such well-built properties commanded ensured it would quickly become the middle-class estate it has remained to this day.

The LCC built around 10,000 council homes before 1914.

1919 HOUSING AND TOWN PLANNING ACT (ADDISON ACT)

For the first time, there were direct central government subsidies available to local authorities to provide for the housing needs in their districts, and give substantial financial assistance to enable them to charge rents working-class families could afford. Housing Associations were also eligible for government subsidies under the scheme.

SUBSIDY ARRANGEMENTS SHARED THE COST OF NEW HOUSING BETWEEN THE TREASURY, THE LOCAL RATES AND THE TENANTS' RENTAL INCOME. THIS ENABLED LOCAL AUTHORITIES TO BEGIN A WIDESPREAD CONSTRUCTION PROGRAMME TO BUILD

'HOMES FIT FOR HEROES'.

THE AIM WAS TO BUILD 500,000 HOUSES IN THREE YEARS.

From 1919 the term 'public housing' was taken to mean any housing provided with the help of government subsidies and local authority funding.

In this post-war period there were widespread fears that the new and worrying spread of Bolshevism would bring about revolution in Britain as it had done in Russia in 1917.

Trade union membership had doubled, the Labour Party had emerged as a powerful force in post-war political life and there had been serious industrial unrest in industry and on the docks throughout the war.

The success of the 1915 Glasgow Rent Strike had forced the government to enforce rent controls – itself an example of unprecedented state interference with market forces.

A Ministry of Reconstruction, aimed at rebuilding national life, was created and public housing came under state control. The first housing manuals were also issued by the Ministry of Health for local authority and others providing social housing.

A lot of post-war housing was built by the governments own Office of Works and was considered then and now as examples of high-quality public housing.

LCC: Ossulston Estate
Chief Architect: G. Topham Forest.
built
1927 - 1931

Following the end of WW1, LCC redeveloped slum housing in this part of Somers Town to rehouse those poor who were not being served by the LCC's new suburban estates.

Consequently, it was much denser. Levita House had the first central heating system to be installed by the LCC.

The design, by G. Topham Forrest, was influenced by Viennese modernist public housing, such as Karl Marx-Hof which he had visited . All the original parts of the estate are now Grade 2 listed buildings.

The LCC's Chief Architect, Topham Forrest, had visited the famed Karl Marx-Hof in Vienna and had been impressed by its achievements.

He concluded the only way he could use the land obtained for building the new estate was by going up higher than 5 storeys despite the fact this would entail additional expense on lifts.

He envisaged a mixed estate for both working class council tenants and private tenants and a range of social facilities and commercial premises that would offset some of the expenditure.

There was no question that the 'superior' private flats should be segregated from the shops and working-class flats.

In the end the private accommodation was dropped and six storeys of exclusively working-class flats were built.

The design of the building with its steel frame construction, precast concrete walls and floors and an external skin of brickwork unadorned walls, reinforced concrete balconies remained as an example of alternative ways of thinking about more modernist public housing building.

1924 HOUSING ACT (FINANCIAL PROVISIONS) ACT

IN ITS 1918 MANIFESTO THE LABOUR PARTY HAD CALLED 1924 HOUSING ACT

In its 1918 Manifesto the Labour Party had called for the immediate building of a million new homes at the at the State's expense fit for men and women to live in and let at fair rents. The demands for slum clearance and rehousing was central to the Labour Party's increasing popularity. Boroughs like Bermondsey and St. Pancras gradually became Labour strongholds with a strong commitment to providing housing and amenities to its working class residents.

LABOUR'S 1924 HOUSING ACT PUT COUNCIL HOUSING CENTRE STAGE AND PRODUCED 493,000 HOMES.

The LCC was one of the few authorities who could afford to build houses taking into account the shortage of materials and a skilled workforce. The LCC realised that many people wanted to live in the centre of London so resumed building flats in inner London which accorded with national policy. Between 1925-1929 they also experimented with 'high rise' housing schemes. High rise meaning up to 5 storeys without lift access. What was considered a reasonable number of levels mainly for women carrying shopping to walk up.

The pioneering experiments in municipal housing in Vienna may have influenced the building of the Estate in Somers Town (built between 1927-1931). As a monument to civic socialism, it cannot be compared. Despite an emerging modernist architectural style based on European models the country cottage with front and back garden model still seen as the ideal.

St. Pancras Housing Association Estates
Architect: Ian Hamilton
1926 – late 1930's

Magdalen College (Oxford) Mission was founded in 1896 and moved to Somers Town in 1908.

It established Clubs for boys and girls, helped people emigrate to Australia, ran a soup kitchen and established a Nursery School. In 1921 a young Anglican priest, Basil Jellicoe (1899 – 1935) was appointed Magdalen Missioner, to be joined soon after by Percy Maryon-Wilson, Edith Neville and Irene Barclay. Together they founded the St. Pancras House Improvement Society in 1924. (eventually to become St. Pancras Housing Association and now Origin HA). Father Jellicoe was a tireless campaigner for the right of poor people to live in well designed and affordable housing, and used his work in Somers Town to demonstrate how this could be achieved.

At first, the Society repaired and renovated slum housing, but soon found that it was so unhealthy, and had deteriorated so far, as to make renovation impractical.

In 1926, therefore, the Society began a demolition / new build programme aimed at re housing as many people as possible in self contained flats often around an inner courtyard. The new housing, which may have been the first voluntary scheme of its type put up after World War I, was let at low rents affordable to unskilled tenants of the slums being replaced - unlike the rents of Council housing in the area which were only affordable to skilled workers. By the end of the 1930's the Housing Association had provided over 600 new homes.

1930 HOUSING ACT

This re-defined the criteria for the selection of slum clearance areas and imposed on local authorities the obligation to rehouse all those displaced by slum clearance schemes. This incentivised slum clearance programmes.

High rises like Ossulston became more popular. (Another example Penshurst now part of the St. Silas & Southfleet Estate) built in 1939 as a high rise by St. Pancras.

1935 HOUSING ACT

This defined what constituted overcrowded living conditions, and obliged local authorities to survey the extent of overcrowding in their areas and prepare plans for sufficient accommodation.

1.1 MILLION NEW COUNCIL HOMES WERE BUILT IN THE 20 YEARS BETWEEN 1919-1939 BUT MOST OF THESE WERE FOR THE MORE AFFLUENT WORKING CLASS WHITE COLLAR OR SKILLED WORKERS WHILE THE MUCH POORER WORKING CLASS WERE STILL LIVING IN SLUMS.

1944 HOUSING (TEMPORARY ACCOMMODATION) ACT

This made provision for £150 million to be expended nationally on the manufacture and erection of temporary homes (prefabs), many of which lasted until well over the 10 years they were originally designed for. A number of these prefabs still survive - a testament to their durability.

The post-war story is one of the creation of the Welfare State and housing policy being a political football between Labour and Conservative.

LABOUR SAW COUNCIL HOUSING AS SERVING A CROSS SECTION OF SOCIETY WHEREAS THE CONSERVATIVES SAW IT AS THE SAFETY NET FOR THE MOST VULNERABLE WHO COULD NOT ASPIRE TO THE PREFERRED IDEAL OF OWNER OCCUPATION.

First resort and last resort – the step up step down theory still prevalent.

It's also the golden period of council house building. Once again it takes

a world war to secure the peace and returning soldiers demanding something better.

The Beveridge Report, published in 1941, was seen as the blueprint for Attlee's Labour Government reforms, had a huge effect on ordinary people, particularly serving soldiers, who were politicised by the war and the report.

It was the 'soldiers' vote that ensured the landslide victory of the Labour Party in 1945 and Labour's promise to Win the Peace. Good quality housing provision, again a central platform of Labour's policies, alongside wide sweeping changes to health, employment, pensions, and education.

IN THE SPIRIT OF THAT POST-WAR WORLD, TOWN PLANNING AND BUILDING CENTRED ON THE CONCEPT OF THE NEIGHBOURHOOD UNIT – REVIVING COMMUNITY FEELING AND ENSURING SOCIAL SOLIDARITY AND SHARED PURPOSE

The post-war world had left massive housing shortages, particularly in London and in areas like St. Pancras and Holborn severely damaged by bombing raids.

1946 LAND ACQUISITION ACT

This enhanced local authorities' ability to compulsorily purchase land and requisition of empty properties to house those in need – a provision Labour councils used extensively.

The County of Land Plan was also introduced outlining a comprehensive redevelopment of London.

St. Pancras Metropolitan Borough Council: Cecil Rhodes House / The Chenies
Architect: Thomas Sibthorp.
Approved in 1949

A very early and ambitious example of post-war Council housing (homes fit for heroes) , these 10/11 storey red brick flats were built in the distinctive Art Deco' style. Much-admired Chenies in 8 storeys' and Cecil Rhodes is 10 storeys (photo).

The LCC built 13 new out-of-county estates in a ring round the capital – the New Town Programme. This was halted by the Conservatives when they came to power in 1951.

Nye Bevan, the committed socialist Minister for Health and Housing, said new council schemes should not be seen just in terms of how many were built but how well they were built.

'WHILE WE WILL BE JUDGED FOR A YEAR BY THE NUMBER OF HOUSES WE BUILD ....WE SHALL BE JUDGED IN TEN YEARS' TIME BY THE TYPE OF HOUSES WE BUILD'[1]

Nye Bevan insisted on larger council houses being built with modern kitchens and gas and electric heating and cookers.

The most important aspects of post-war planning were neighbourhood units, mixed developments and the separation of cars and pedestrians. Bevan was also anxious there would be no segregation of different income groups .

COUNCIL HOUSING SHOULD NOT BE JUST FOR THE POOR. THE DOCTOR, BAKER AND POSTMAN COULD ALL LIVE IN THE SAME STREET. 804,921 COUNCIL HOUSES WERE BUILT UNDER LABOUR BETWEEN 1945-51.

This was impressive, given post-war economic conditions and labour shortages.

1951 CONSERVATIVE GOVERNMENT IN POWER.

Harold Macmillan, the Minister of Housing, promised 300,000 more homes annually, and by 1953 had

1   Quoted in Boughton, J (2018) Municipal Dreams p. 94 London, Verso

surpassed this figure. However, there was a sharp reduction in council house quality and space standards.

The government continued to promote and encourage house building for owner occupiers. It also favoured high-density standardised high rises often shoddily built and could quickly meet the needs of severe housing shortages.

1954 HOUSING ACT

This obliged local authorities to estimate their slum problems and submit proposals for dealing with them. It required future council efforts to concentrate on redevelopment and slum clearance.

It also exempted properties belonging to housing associations from rent control.

St. Pancras Metropolitan Borough Council: Godwin and Crowndale Estate.
Built in the mid 1950's

Fronting onto Crowndale Road, these two substantial red brick 8/9 storey blocks were built on the site of houses badly damaged during WW2. They provide a total of 173 flats with a series of car parking and grassed courtyard areas, fenced football / kickabout area and small community garden to the rear. The street frontage to Crowndale Court provides local shopping, while the Al-Rahman Mosque and Community Centre is located to the rear of Godwin Court.

1956 HOUSING SUBSIDIES ACT

This revised government subsidies so that local authority efforts were concentrated on redevelopment rather than general housing need. It increased the subsidy on high rises and encouraged the growing trend for local authorities to rehouse in high rise blocks.

The Act also abolished the statutory obligation of councils to pay a fixed contribution to the rates the intention being to encourage them to charge 'realistic 'rents for their council housing.

This resulted in a 1960 St. Pancras

Rent Strike[2]

THE 1958 MAY DAY RED FLAG INCIDENT INVOLVED JOHN LAWRENCE, LEADER OF ST PANCRAS COUNCIL HOISTING THE RED FLAG FROM TOWN HALL [3]

Lawrence, who lived in Ossulston Estate, was arrested at the May Day Rally.

This indicated community support and involvement in the rent strikes and the role John Lawrence and the labour group on St. Pancras Council played in trying to stop the rent increases.

The lack of building sites, particularly in London, and the increasing cost of land left little alternatives other than building higher. It was also a cheap way of building not just for housing, but also for schools, hospitals, universities. It added to the characterisation of council housing as vast estates of Brutalist high-rise blocks.

HOME OWNERSHIP WAS STILL BEING ENCOURAGED AND EVEN THE LABOUR PARTY MANIFESTO PROPOSED THE RIGHT TO BUY FOR SITTING COUNCIL TENANTS IN ITS 1959 MANIFESTO

Regent's Park Estate was built in this period
The 19-storey tower block on estate was described as the tallest residential building to be built in London since the war. The original Regency style houses had fallen into disrepair or been demolished in air raids. St. Pancras acquired properties owned by the Crown Estate and compulsory purchased remaining houses. In 1944 Eric Cook, Vice Chair of St. Pancras Borough Labour Party said that most had been built by Regency jerry builders and could be used to create working class flats:

'FOR THE MAIN BULK AND BACKBONE OF OUR PEOPLE'.

The Ronan Point gas explosion in

1968 which triggered the collapse of a corner of the tower exposed the shocking building defects, and the poor quality control governing the system-built high rises. With the removal of subsidies, their popularity decreased and from then on there was a clear preference for low rise developments.

In the decade from 1968-1979 some of best council housing was built, in contrast to the idea that badly planned, high-rise estates built in dangerous locales was the norm for council housing.

Camden Council was a leader in the field from its creation in 1965. Notable architects were Neave Brown, Benson & Forsyth, Peter Tabori. Neave Brown was the only UK architect to be Grade Listed for all of his designs.

1972 – 1974 4 HOUSING ACTS

These acts abandoned the concept of the fair rent. Councils could charge a reasonable rent at their own discretion. The responsibility for the provision of public housing shifted from local authorities to housing associations.

HOUSING (HOMELESS PERSONS) ACT 1977

This imposed a statutory duty on local authorities to provide accommodation for certain groups of the homeless.

Whilst well-intentioned, ultimately this had unintended consequences in that it increasingly reserved council housing for the least well off and the most vulnerable, and not for general need. It altered the composition of mixed communities and created a range of social problems that were forever associated only with council housing.

At the same time the drive to owner occupation was becoming increasingly popular.

The election of Margaret Thatcher's radical Conservative government oversaw the largest privatisation of public assets ever with the introduction of the 1980 Right to Buy Rent Act.

---

2   St. Pancras Chronicle 8 Jan 1960
3   St. Pancras Chronicle 2 May 1958 & 9 May 1958

1980 RIGHT TO BUY RENT ACT

The Right to Buy had been favoured by Conservative councils since the 1920s but was an option very few councils actively encouraged. There would have been little take up.

Ironically, the working classes, who had benefited from the availability of employment, free health care and education, saw it as an opportunity to climb the housing ladder.

It has been calculated that 40% of the council stock of housing sold is now in the hands of private landlords, who in turn, rent these properties at unaffordable rents and even back to the very councils who built them.

The government's intention was to shift tenure of Britain's housing stock to owner occupiers, diminish the role of local authorities in housing provision and effectively end council housing for all but the most needy.

TREASURY RECEIPTS FOR THE SALE OF COUNCIL PROPERTIES STAYED WITH THE TREASURY TO CLEAR DEBT. THERE WAS NO PRETENCE THAT IT WOULD BE USED TO BUILD MORE HOUSES.[4]

The state was painted as the enemy of freedom, making tenants unwilling or unable to move as they dependent on the state for all their needs. Critics inferred a sapping of the spirit, just as had been inferred when council housing was first introduced.

Conservative and even New Labour policies in the 1980s and 1990s cast local authorities as poor landlords, and assumed Housing Associations could do better.

JACKIE LEWIS IS A RESEARCHER AND ARCHIVIST
MICHAEL PARKES IS A TOWN PLANNER WHO WORKED IN SOMERS TOWN

LB Camden Oakshott Court
Architect: Peter Tabori and Roman Halter Associates / James Gowan
1969 – 1971 / 1976

The original Polygon was replaced in 1894 by Polygon Buildings: 4 parallel blocks of railway workers flats, which, over the years, fell below modern housing standards and were, in turn, replaced by Oakshott Court.

Peter Tabori's design was based on his Highgate New Town scheme. Pedestrians and vehicles are segregated. The highly unusual stepped back chevron plan allows for maximum daylight and sunlight to all flats.

LB Camden: Monica Shaw Court
Designed for Camden Community Housing Association
Architect: Gerd Kaufmann and Jim Scott Partnership 1969 – 1971
Built by LB Camden 1975 – 1978

The site had been occupied by the Hampden Club and railwayman's hostel. It formed part of a 2.1 acre island site shared with Phoenix Court, a St. Pancras HA housing estate.

The brief was complex – as well as housing it included a Community Hall and pre–school Nursery, plus car parking at a 1 – 1 ratio. The scheme comprised, to the north, a pair of 6 storey buildings, the longer of which, facing Polygon Road , included 2 floors for the Nursery to the west, a 4 storey building end – on to Ossulston Street containing the Community Hall (STCA) with flats above and, to the south, a pair of 3 to 4 storey buildings end – on to Brill Place with a landscaped court between them.

Access to the upper units was by access decks employing Scott's 'Housing design reference' in the process.

LB Camden: Coopers Lane Estate
Architect: Director of Technical Services / Project Architect: Mike Purdy.
Landscape Architect: Michael Brown Partnership.
Built 1978-81

A detailed Planning Brief 1975 culminated in purchase and development of this former Railway Coal Depot by Camden Borough Council. The bulk of the site (1.5ha) is laid out along semi-Radburn lines, i.e. mainly 2 – 4-storey terraced housing / flats either side of, and fronting onto, a largely pedestrian N-S through route with accompanying hard and soft landscaping. Cars and other vehicles are consigned to the eastern edge of the development.

In total there are 169 units ranging from 1 to 5 bed. The estate includes a block of 46 Warden supported units for the elderly (with lift) together with a number of ground floor flats and houses specially designed for the disabled. Many of the properties have private gardens, others have balconies. These properties back up immediately onto / overlook the remainder of the site (0.4ha) which was originally known as Somers Green. This is designated Public Open Space, and is currently an attractive pocket park with many mature trees.

LB Camden: Mayford Estate
Architect: Eric Lyons designed 1971

Having worked for Walter Gropius and Maxwell Fry, Eric Lyons (1912-1980) co-founded the development company Span in 1948, along with Geoffrey Townsend and Leslie Bilsby. Much of his work was carried out in a suburban context. Schemes such as the Mayford Estate necessarily had to be denser in form and layout (including underground car parking).

Nevertheless, Mayford broadly illustrates the Span ideals of generous communal landscaping and modern brick building.

4   Quoted from John Boughton 'Municipal Dreams: The Rise and Fall of Council Housing'

LEVITA HOUSE

THE HUMANITY OF AESTHETICS

BY SYLVIE TEMPLE

Levita House is situated in Somers Town, an area that was once part of the old St. Pancras borough but now falls within Camden's boundaries and governance - it is acknowledged by conservationists, architects and many who simply walk by as a singularly unique building.

English Heritage refers to Levita House and its neighbouring buildings as the most important interwar estate in the UK reflecting as it does the new and progressive design ethos emerging in the early 20th Century and developed after WWI that sought to ally social and political ideals within a functional aesthetic. Levita House, completed in 1930, is a prime example of this Bauhausian thinking, whereby design and function held equal importance – and applied as it was (uniquely) to a London County Council housing estate made it a truly pioneering project.

Levita House stands alone architecturally in Somers Town. Although it formed part of the slum clearance work instigated initially by the great efforts of Rev Basil Jellicoe, it shifted the focus away from any religious symbolism or allegiance, sharpening its lens instead upon a very different utopia.

It is an extraordinarily imposing structure with importance given from the outset to trees and landscaping and it is clear that both George Topham Forrest, chief architect for the LCC and Cecil Levita, chairman of the housing committee, in arriving at their final design were powerfully influenced by a similar scheme in Vienna called Karl -Marx Hof. This inspiration partly explains the high gabled roofs which appear to be an anomaly, calling, as they

do, on a more arts and crafts sensibility. But even they are functional, allowing for the top floor flats to have a second internal floor whilst the building itself complied with the five-story limit without a lift, which was the rule.

The building as with its Viennese cousin is a long arched design (although the Hof is 3 kilometres overall, which Levita cannot claim!) – it is fascinating in the diversity of its structural choices. It appears austere initially:

WHEN I FIRST SAW IT IN THE FADING LIGHT OF AN EARLY WINTERS DUSK I WAS LITERALLY MESMERISED – NOT SURE WHETHER TO BE ENTHRALLED OR TERRIFIED

But as I have come to explore it more, I have found also the additional surface detailing with softening 1930's motifs and heard from elderly residents about other decorative elements long lost – the colourful LCC insignia and green painted windows and doors.

The modernist angularity of the design was matched in its modernity by the first full internal electrification (for public housing) and a system, which allowed hot water to be pumped separately to both baths and other utilities internally.

These kinds of amenities were pivotal to the ethos of the building - no longer would such basic human rights be denied. It is no surprise therefore that Levita House architecturally and as a social model is still lectured on in architectural schools across the UK, Historic England consider it to be of extreme importance and

The Twentieth Century Society, acknowledged as the experts in buildings of this era, have been strongly engaged with its protection since 2016.

I suggest it was certainly also well-known and respected by the architects who ran Camden Council's pioneering architectural department in the 1960's, whose buildings so proudly took up the cause and who, consequently, created so many landmark estates across the borough. Many of them also listed and all imbued with the humanity of their aesthetic and intent.

does, to an area of unusually vital early and mid twentieth century architectural history, which altogether tells an extraordinary story.

SOMERS TOWN UNIQUELY CONTAINS - WITHIN ONE SMALL AREA OF CENTRAL LONDON - AN EXTRAORDINARILY IMPORTANT COLLECTION OF PIONEERING SOCIAL HOUSING DESIGN SPANNING SEVERAL DECADES.

SYLVIA TEMPLE, LEVITA HOUSE RESIDENT AND MEMBER OF THE TWENTIETH CENTURY SOCIETY

So Levita House is clearly a marker in what ought to be a proud legacy for Camden. It certainly was an innovative building in its day, and holds a very particular place in social history.

Having advocated for this extraordinary building now for several years, I suggest its social, historic and architectural importance powerfully contribute to the case for Somers Town being granted conservation status.

The addition of a local conservation area, although it should not take precedence over individual listed buildings protection, would provide Levita House with some much deserved further sanctuary - adding, as it

Karl Marx Hof, Vienna

Photos Diana Foster, and London Metropolitan Archives (above).

RENT STRIKE

ST PANCRAS

BY JOHN COWLEY

If class conflict has any relevance to the making of history, then the St. Pancras Rent Strike of 1960 is an outstanding example.

It was an extraordinary episode in Post-War Britain. It brought people on to the streets of St. Pancras, in a display of demonstrations, marches and rallies, in a show of energy and enthusiasm, an expression of spirit. So dazzling, it ranks with May 1968 and other such historic moments. It was much more localised than the Paris events, in a relatively compact inner London borough, but for those who participated, it was an unforgettable moment in their lives:

'WHAT A DAY!" SAYS FLO BURGESS, "WHAT A DAY!'

The events unfolded over a number of days, bringing people together, in association, on the streets, sharing an exhilarating moment, a sense of festival. For those involved, the days are equivalent to years. They refused to live as was expected of them.

It is a story worth telling.

The early stages of Britain's post-war recovery were presided over by a Labour Government steeped in notions of social justice forged in the early part of the century. By 1951 the Tories had returned to office. Towards the end of the 1950s, with the Cold War fractured by events of 1956 – the 20th Congress of the CPSU and its intervention in Hungary and the British/French humiliation in Suez – a radical Labour Council was elected in the inner London Borough of St. Pancras.

It raised the banner of municipal socialism, flying the red flag on the Town Hall roof, giving staff a holiday on May Day, not increasing the rents of council tenants, refusing to pay the civil defence levy, and generally pursuing a programme intended to benefit working class people.

It was too radical for the Labour Party, led by Hugh Gaitskell, so some of the most militant Councillors were expelled from the Labour Party. Simultaneously the Conservative Government surcharged Councillors for refusing to raise rents. A divided Council was swept out of power and a Conservative Council elected.

A new means-tested rent scheme was introduced. This met with furious opposition from a roused working class. The local Trades Council, union branches, tenants' associations, local party branches of the Labour and Communist Parties all became involved. A rent strike was organised with widespread local support.

The crucial issue was the Conservative Government's 1957 Rent Act. The Act removed many of the limits placed on the rent levels of private tenancies. It helped usher in a new era of property speculation in the private rented sector, opening the way for the, at the time, notorious developer and landlord Peter Rachman in Notting Hill. Henceforth rents were to be related to rateable value.

St. Pancras Council undertook to pay the increase for tenants living in de-requisitioned properties. This broke the rules governing local authority finances. As a consequence, the District Auditor surcharged 23 Councillors. They were held legally responsible for the 'misspent' public monies. The Labour Party nationally disowned the rebel Councillors and, in the summer of 1958, John Lawrence, Charles Taylor and twelve other Councillors were expelled from the Labour Party. Their views were considered to be:

'INDISTINGUISHABLE FROM THOSE OF KNOWN COMMUNISTS'.

They formed an Independent Labour Group of Councillors.[1]

The local Labour Party was split down the middle by the expulsions and the Conservatives gained control of the Council in the local elections in May 1959. The new Tory Council introduced a means-tested rent scheme for all of its own tenants. 'Rents-according-to-income' met with widespread resistance.

Tenants formed themselves into the St. Pancras United Tenants Association. Meetings and marches were held demanding withdrawal of the increases. A petition signed by 16,000 people was rejected by the Council. In January 1960 the rent increases were introduced. The United Tenants Association, consisting of 35 affiliated associations, organised a borough-wide withholding of the rent increase.

Some 8,000 tenants were involved in the rent strike.

'AT THE HEIGHT OF THE STRUGGLE THE UTA TOOK OUT EVERY NIGHT AS MANY AS 60 WOMEN, BANGING ON THE COUNCILLORS' DOORS.

If a councillor did not get two visits a week he was lucky; as one UTA leader put it:

'WE SENT THEIR WIVES UP THE WALL.'

It was a tactic that paid off.

1   See Camden Tenant, 94, Winter 1985. Image of strike leader Dan Cook barricaded in his Kenniston House home in Kentish Town.

THE POLICE WERE LESS LIKELY TO ARREST THE WOMEN AND WOMEN THEMSELVES WERE KEEN. IT WASN'T DIFFICULT FOR THE AVERAGE HOUSEWIFE TO REALISE SHE WAS IN TROUBLE WITH THE RENT RISES. MOST OF THE WOMEN DIDN'T GO TO WORK THEN.THEY FORMED THE BACKBONE OF THE MOVEMENT, KEEPING EVERYTHING GOING IN THE DAY AND GIVING EACH OTHER MUTUAL SUPPORT.' [2]

A number of tenants living on the St. Pancras Way estate and in Camelot House to the North of Camden Square were active in withholding the rent increase. The women regularly attended meetings of the UTA and joined in the nightly campaigning. The Council threatened to evict those tenants withholding rent.

In June, the Bloomsbury County Court served eviction notices on three tenants, recognised as leaders of the campaign. One of these was Don Cook who lived nearby in Kennistoun House in Leighton Road, Kentish Town. Don's father and brother ran the J C Motor Supplies in Murray Street, close to Camden Square, and so the family were well known and respected in the neighbourhood.

The Council issued a further 240 notices to quit. Protest meetings and demonstrations were held throughout the Borough. The local branch of the National Union of Railwaymen held a two-hour strike. Building workers formed a flying picket in readiness to resist eviction. Don Cook and Arthur Rowe, two leaders of the resistance, barricaded themselves in their respective flats. At the September Council meeting a number of protesting tenants were arrested and taken into custody. The next day:

SEPT'EMBER 22ND AT 5 AM BAILIFFS WITH 800 POLICE IN SUPPORT SMASHED THEIR WAY INTO SILVERDALE, REGENTS PARK ESTATE, AND KENNISTON HOUSE EVICTING ARTHUR ROWE AND DON COOK AND HIS FAMILY.'

At both sites there were pitched battles between tenants and police.[3]

Flo Burgess who had lived on the St. Pancras Way Estate, since the first flats were completed in 1948, remembered vividly the events of that day. When ever asked about the day of the evictions Flo was want to proclaim: 'What a day!'

Woken up shortly after 5 am by a young boy running the length of the balcony, swinging a football rattle above his head, Flo and her husband joined with their neighbours and walked quickly to the scene of the eviction. Many on the St. Pancras Way Estate were withholding their rent. Some

were members of the Labour Party, and considered themselves to be Labour families.

They went together to Don Cook's and participated in the demonstration. That day Flo went late to the tailors where she worked part-time. Hundreds of men and women converged on Leighton Road. The courtyard of Kennistoun House filled with demonstrating tenants, including Don Cook and his wife, Edie. Hundreds of police were present. A thunderous cheer went up when building workers from the Shell Mex site, down by the Thames, arrived, having marched up Kentish Town Road.

Skirmishes broke out between demonstrators and police. Men and women sat down in the road. Similar scenes were being enacted on the Regent Park Estate, following the eviction of Arthur Rowe.

The extraordinary events of 22 September were quite against the grain of conventional politics at that time. It was a moment of class war: an act of insubordination. There were street battles with tenants and supporting building and railway workers, culminating that evening, the day of the evictions, with thousands of protestors marching down the Euston Road to the Town Hall. Over 1,000 police confronted the demonstrators, as they tried to disperse the crowd bus and car windows were broken, dozens were injured, including police and there were numerous arrests.

The St. Pancras Chronicle reported next day:

Police with batons drawn charged again and again into hordes of screaming, fighting rent rebels at St. Pancras last night. Scores of injured demonstrators and police were carried off by a shuttle service of ambulances as the astonishing battle raged. Cars were stoned, trolley-bus windows smashed. The rioting crowd matched police batons with sticks, milk bottles, rocks – even eggs. Men, women and children were trampled under the rush of determined constables. Policemen knocked off their feet were kicked and beaten. Men punched, wrestled, clawed and clutched. They rolled and roared, women screamed and scratched, in a mob fury unmatched by anything anyone could remember. The Battle of St. Pancras flared when 2,000 rent rebels marched on St. Pancras Town Hall after a three-hour meeting outside Kennistoun House, in Leighton Road, Kentish Town, where council tenant Don Cook had been forcibly evicted from his council flat. [4]

After the strike was over, many of the participants retained an overwhelming sense of achievement. Jim Duggan, recently arrived from Waterford in Ireland with his family, was one of those who marched that day.

Three lines of policemen stood across Euston Road to stop the marchers from reaching the Town Hall. Injured by the

2 Dave Burn, Rent Strike: St. Pancras

3 Camden Tenant, 94, Winter 1985.

4 St. Pancras Chronicle, 23 September 1960.

1960, Pluto, London, 1972, p 8

police, Jim was carried to safety by fellow demonstrators and, despite the shock and pain to his injured leg, he found the whole experience exhilarating.

Together they had stood up to the authorities on a matter of principle. Arthur Rowe and Don Cook, the evicted leaders of the strike, were local heroes.

'THE RENT STRUGGLE' SAID CHARLES TAYLOR, THE FORMER REBEL COUNCILLOR, 'WAS A FIRST EXERCISE IN COMMUNITY AFFAIRS'[5].

It was an example of communities maintaining solidarity and localised support for a particular cause: the sense of belonging to a particular locality, a place, was all the stronger.

But for Edie Cook, it was a day of misery: the loss of the family's home darkened her life for some considerable time. Well over forty years after the event, she still remembered the deep hurt of that day.

JOHN COWLEY IS AN ACADEMIC, HISTORIAN AND LIVES IN AGAR GROVE

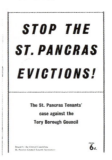

STOP THE
ST. PANCRAS
EVICTIONS!

The St. Pancras Tenants'
case against the
Tory Borough Council

6d.

---

5   Camden Tenant, 94, Winter 1985.

Images courtesy of Councillor Roger Robinson, who took part in the strike, from his friend Don Cook.

STOP THIS SAVAGE ATTACK ON ST PANCRAS FAMILIES !

AN APPEAL TO NON BOROUGH COUNCIL TENANTS

The Tories on St Pancras Borough Council have INCREASED the rents of Borough Council flats by amounts ranging from 10/- to £3 a week.   To live in some Council flats after January 4th will cost the tenant as much as £5. 6. 5. a week !   Adding insult to injury there is also to be a MEANS TEST investigation into the incomes of those who can't afford these staggering rent increases.

Council tenants are up in arms.   They are forming Tenants Associations all over the Borough to resist the rent increases, and it is up to workers who are NOT council tenants to give them all the help they can.

TYPICAL TORY TRICKERY

The Tories say they are imposing these huge rent increases so as to wipe out the rate subsidy for Council Housing and thus save YOU - the ordinary ratepayers of the Borough - a lot of money. This is typical Tory trickery.   They omit to tell you that what you pay in rates depends on the rateable value of the house or flat in which you live, or the size of your business in the Borough.   Those who live in the worst conditions pay the smallest contribution to the Housing subsidy and consequently have little or nothing to gain from this wicked attack on Council tenants.

If, for example, you live in a pre-war L.C.C. flat in Somerstown or in a pre-war flat built by the St Pancras Housing Association, this new Rent Scheme will save you about four PENCE a week in rates. But if you live in a large house in one of the "select" parts of the Borough (where, incidentally the Leader of the Tory Council lives the rent increases for Council tenants will save you about four SHILLINGS a week in rates.   And if you happen to own a large factory, a chain-store, or a big block of offices, the attack on Council tenants will profit you to the extent of four POUNDS a week and more in rates !   So you see, it isn't the ordinary ratepayer whom the Tories are helping.   It is the big businessmen of the Borough - the people who finance the Tories.

Is it right that working people living in Council flats should be hit over the head with these enormous rent increases so that the rich industrial and commercial interests in the Borough can have their rates substantially reduced ?

WHO IS RESPONSIBLE FOR THE HIGH COST OF HOUSING ?

It is not the Borough Council tenants who are responsible for the present deficit on the Housing Account.   It is the Tory Government which has stopped all State housing subsidies and forced

Below Cllr. Roger Robinson who took part in the Rent Strike.

GOLDEN AGE

"effective housing policy...at rents you can afford."

- Enid Wistrich, Local Government Reorganisations, The First
Years of Camden. (London Borough of Camden, 1972)

Phyllis Hodges, Lord Goodman and dignitaries visit a tenant in her flat in Edith Neville Cottages, April 16th 1975.
Photo from St. Pancras Housing collection.
Courtesy of Camden Local Studies and Archives Centre.

HILL HOUSING

IN SOMERS TOWN

BY FABIAN WATKINSON

Somers Town is flat.

Yet in its midst lies a remarkable group of housing which carries the flavour of an Italian hill town. Designed by an émigré from the 1956 Hungarian Revolution, taken over by a Polish survivor of Auschwitz and finally completed by a leading Scottish architect, Oakshott Court is a striking example of the designs created by Camden Architects' Department under Borough Architect Sydney Cook in the 1960s and '70s.

Other notable estates include Fleet Road and Alexandra Road (by Neave Brown and both listed); Branch Hill (also listed), Mansfield Road/Lamble Street and Maiden Lane (by Gordon Benson and Alan Forsyth); and Highgate New Town (by Peter Tábori).

These belong to a brief golden era when many architects fought for their belief that nothing was too good for social housing, using modern materials to create light-filled and exciting interior spaces – an era which was ended by the period of inflation, the growing reaction against Modernism of the seventies and Margaret Thatcher's drastic curb on local authority spending.

We are therefore unlikely to see public housing on this scale of such high quality again in the foreseeable future. As the architect John Winter put it: '

BETWEEN THE SYSTEM BUILDING SPREE OF THE SIXTIES AND THE LATE SEVENTIES SLIDE INTO FOLKSINESS THERE WAS A MAGICAL MOMENT FOR ENGLISH HOUSING WHEN EMINENTLY HABITABLE PLACES OF CLARITY AND CALM WERE DESIGNED AND BUILT … CAMDEN HAS CONTRIBUTED RICHLY TO THIS SCENE.'

On 1 May 1965, the Metropolitan Boroughs of Hampstead (affluent, genteel and Conservative), Holborn (a place of work rather than homes) and St. Pancras (mainly working-class and Labour) became the London Borough of Camden. Described by some as a shotgun wedding, apart from the City of London and the City of Westminster, and thanks to the business rates from Holborn, Camden was by far the wealthiest new local authority in London.

It saw itself as a flagship and soon gained a reputation as also being the most radical. As Borough Architect, it appointed the fifty-five-year-old Sydney Cook, who had held the same position at Holborn.

SYDNEY COOK

Sydney cook

Cook designed little himself for Camden but built up a formidable team of mainly young architects. Housing was at the top of the political agenda, the accepted solution being system-built high-rise. Cook's alternative was for low-rise developments (rarely more than four storeys) with a high density (about 200 people per acre).

During his era the Architects' Department resisted the enormous pressure from the government and the planners; it never used industrialised building techniques and didn't build a single tower block. Cook always said: 'I'll use standardised plans if you can find me a standardised site.'

In order to get officials to accept these projects he had to have a persuasive manner. Once he believed in one of his young architects' schemes, he did his utmost to ensure it was built as designed, always appearing before the council to defend it.

PETER TÁBORI

Peter Tábori joined Camden Architects' Department in 1968, after being headhunted by Cook. Born in Hungary in 1940, he was imprisoned as a 'class enemy' when the Russians invaded in 1956. After six months he was suddenly released and was able to join his family who had escaped to England, where he was granted asylum and, later, citizenship.

He studied at the Regent Street Polytechnic (now the University of Westminster), where his teachers included Neave Brown (who received the Royal Institute of British Architects Gold Medal in 2017) and Richard Rogers (now Lord Rogers), spending two years out working with fellow-Hungarian Ernö Goldfinger, whose house in Hampstead is now owned by the National Trust. He then worked for three years with Denys Lasdun (architect of the National Theatre), mainly on the University of East Anglia.

Tábori's first project at Camden was the rebuilding of Highgate New Town, next to Highgate Cemetery, but when the compulsory purchase orders were delayed Cook asked him to look at another site, Polygon Road (now Oakshott Court) in Somers Town.

Peter Tábori

network of stairs, ingeniously creating the illusion of a hill town. And as each terrace steps down a storey, most get a view of the green.

Tábori wanted to create a modern version of the traditional street with through routes, not an estate cut off from the world around. His models included not only the hill towns of northern Italy, which he had visited on the advice of his Italian-born teacher, Richard Rogers, but also mining villages and Georgian terraces.

Every flat had its own front door opening onto the street, creating a clear distinction between public and private space, the original design having no lifts or communal access. And at the junction of the terraces at each level there was a small public square, or piazza, originally intended as a play area so that every child could play close to home.

The 114 dwellings have a surprising variety of layouts, from one-bedroom flats to six-person maisonettes. A stepped section gives each flat at least one glazed wall opening onto a balcony or patio with space open to the sky. Maisonettes get two balconies, the larger ones on the upper level even having a third, facing Chalton Street.

THE SITE

The original Polygon, begun by Jacob Leroux in 1791, was an unusual design of sixteen sides around which thirty-two Georgian houses were arranged in pairs. But the area declined rapidly with the coming of the railways, becoming poor and overcrowded, and the Polygon was finally demolished in 1891. It was replaced with Polygon Buildings, four blocks aligned north-south across the site.

Built in recompense for the great loss of housing when St. Pancras Station was constructed in the 1860s, they housed many railway employees. Although austere and barrack-like, when new they were considered to be model dwellings, with two small rooms per family, communal sinks and toilets. But by the 1960s they no longer met modern requirements, so the planners decided it was time to replace them with something better.

THE DESIGN

Based on his work at Highgate, Tábori's design for Oakshott Court consisted of a four-storey terrace embracing two two-storey ones, arranged on five levels.

These are divided at ninety degrees, creating an L-shape, so that every flat gets some southern light. The housing is placed furthest away from the busiest road to the south, taking only two-thirds of the site, the other third being open space. Yet at 220 people per acre the density is still very high.

At Highgate, Tábori was building on a hill: here the site was completely flat. But by placing the top three storeys over the car parks at ground level, and excavating a storey below, he formed pedestrian streets on three levels, connected by a

Divided by private screen walls, these are like outdoor rooms for eating, sitting in the sun and so on, whilst on the road sides the windows are much smaller. And careful thought was given to how the maisonettes would be used by families. All have living rooms on the top floor, to provide light and views, with bedrooms below, whilst the interiors of the two-storey blocks are flooded with light from clerestory windows.

The original design included a community centre above the boiler-house at the junction of the tallest blocks. In the end this corner space was redesigned by the later architects as flats with a lift, creating striking chamfered brick and round towers, with areas of exposed concrete. Camden's planning committee approved Tábori's design in outline in June 1969 and in full in November 1971. By this time his plans for the first stage of Highgate New Town had been approved, and as the Architects' Department was overloaded,

Sydney Cook brought in Roman Halter, an outside architect who had worked with his deputy, Peter Clapham, at Haringey. Halter, whose job was to supervise the

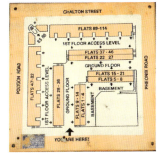

construction of Oakshott Court, made one significant change. Tábori's design was to be built of sand-coloured precast concrete panels and matching blockwork, as at Highgate. Much to his annoyance, Halter changed this to red brick, in deference, he said, to St. Pancras station nearby.

Sadly, Cook became ill with leukaemia and left Camden in 1973. His successor, Alfred Rigby, was a totally different character, dismantling the department that Cook had so carefully built up. He hated concrete and loved brick. 'Brick was my nemesis', lamented Tábori later.

ROMAN HALTER

Born in 1927, Roman Halter was only twelve when the Nazis took over Chodecz, the village in Northern Poland where he grew up. As Jews, he and his family were sent to Auschwitz where he spent his adolescence witnessing the worst horrors of human history. His family were killed but Roman survived, coming to England in 1945, where he had a successful career as an architect. In Camden, he designed a home for the elderly in Wellesley Road, Gospel Oak, a sensitive and humane project in red brick, sadly now replaced.

They say that time is a great healer, but it's not always true, particularly for survivors of the Holocaust. In 1973, whilst working on Oakshott Court, Roman's memories suddenly returned with such power that he had to give up his career as an architect. The nightmares recurred for the rest of his life, which he devoted to designing stained glass and painting.

And after decades of silence he spent his last years, until his death in 2012, visiting schools to tell his story. Not to elicit pity or sympathy but to tell the truth, remembering that his grandfather had made him promise that when he survived he would tell people about what he had seen. And he always emphasised that his grandfather had said 'when' not ' if'.

Roman Halter

JAMES GOWAN

After Halter's breakdown, Oakshott Court was seen through to completion by James Gowan, another outside architect. Born in Glasgow in 1923, he studied at the Glasgow School of Art, later teaching at the Architectural Association, Princeton University, the Royal College of Art and University College, London.

He was in partnership with James Stirling from 1956 to 1963; as Stirling and Gowan they shot to fame in the late 1950s with such powerful and original designs as the Langham House flats at Ham Common and the engineering building at Leicester University.

These became some of the most influential buildings of their time. Gowan's many other projects included fine housing schemes in Preston, Greenwich, Essex and the Isle of Wight.

He died in 2015.

James Gowan

Finally completed in May 1976, Oakshott Court was named after William (Bill) Oakshott who had been Mayor of Camden and had died the previous year.

With so much new housing now either high-rise or gated, there are many lessons to be learned from such a remarkable and humane achievement, exceptional for its clarity of form and careful detailing.

FABIAN WATKINSON LIVES IN HIGHGATE NEW TOWN, PETER TÁBORI'S OTHER IMPORTANT ESTATE, AND HAS WRITTEN TWO BOOKLETS ON CAMDEN'S HOUSING FOR THE TWENTIETH CENTURY SOCIETY.

Photo of Pearly King and Queen, Oakshott Court 2019 by Siobhan Bradshaw.

MIMI ROMILLY, SINGER AND ACTIVIST, EX-POLYGON

"I grew up in Somers Town with my mum, as a single mum had a flat at Polygon because she was a railway worker. I later returned here with my young son as shown in the photo where polygon stood - it's now Oakshott Court. Polygon had communal bathrooms and kitchens. I taught here, too. I went into showbusiness and am a singer. I've traced my family back to Leroux and Sir Samuel Romilly.
I campaign against HS2."

Photo by Diana Foster

DANIEL EVERITT, EX-COOPERS LANE ESTATE

"I was born in UCH and my family were from Camden / Somers Town and can be traced back 130 years. I went to St. Marys school, then to William Ellis. We used to play football on the green behind my flat on Coopers Lane. My parents ran the Anchor pub and I drank there as well as the Eastnor and the Jubilee. I miss Somers Town and how it used to be."

Daniel's brother Richard was murdered as a teenager, by gang violence in the 1990s.

Photo by Andy Commons

ALBERT, ST. AUGUSTINE'S HOUSE

"I live here with my family. I run a boxing club for the youth of Somers Town. Boxing helps prevent them getting into gangs. It helped me."

Photo by Andy Commons

AMPTHILL ESTATE

THE COUNTRY IN THE CITY

BY ESTHER LESLIE

The three Ampthill Estate towers loom over the Mornington Crescent end of Camden, the tall blocks like three huge cliffs raised about the sea of life below, or above a soil of busy, non-stop activity.

Perhaps from the heights of the upper floors, the inhabitants of Camden appear as ants.

The name of the estate would suggest something slightly different, that it is the inhabitants of the blocks who are the ants.

The estate is named after the original garden square with terraced houses around a crescent-shaped green patch, which was laid out, in 1800, on part of what is now its footprint. Ampthill Square took its name from the Ampthill town and civil parish in Bedfordshire.

The name has an Anglo-Saxon origin and the first settlement was called 'Aemethyll', which means either 'ant-heap' or 'ant infested hill'. The estate received the name after the square, which received the name because of the ducal house of Bedford, which owned the land in both areas. Ampthill Estate's shadow was the Bedford's estate at Ampthill Park, a great park laid out by Capability Brown in the eighteenth century.

In 1837, the London & Birmingham Railway cut through the fields to the west of the square on its route to Euston. This gash severed the area from the more genteel parts of Regent's Park. A second railway opened in 1850, the North London, and so the square was hemmed in by more smoke and iron clatter.

The London Midland and Scottish Railway Company bought up the square and surrounding land in 1912, chipping away more parts. On Ampthill and neighbouring Harrington Square, the once fine, single family plus servants' houses became dilapidated, beflecked with soot, broken up into multiple flats.

The doctors, dentists and clergymen moved on. A seediness descended on the area over time, one that attracted the attentions of the Camden Town Group painters, Walter Sickert and Spencer Gore, whose subjects were music halls and night life and morally dubious nudes in Mornington Crescent interiors.

But that was long ago. Long ago too the towers shot up, and the lower rise buildings spread out over the site of the Ampthill Estate.

The estate was built 50 years ago, in 1969, by direct municipal labour. And this was 64 years after what might be called the first council flats erected in the area by the then newly formed St. Pancras Borough Council, Goldington Buildings.

By the time the Ampthill Estate was built, council housing was well of age. The towers have half a century behind them, and one significant refurbishment in the late 1980s, when the primary colour coding of yellow, blue and red was introduced and a new cladding added, one that withstood for the most part a fire in 2011, when just two flats were destroyed.

There was also a massive flood in one of the buildings, Gillfoot House, in September 2009, which knocked out the electricity.

To be perverse, for a moment, might one see this as a certain elemental sign, a bursting in of natural forces, an ingress of that sea above which those cliffs of towers rage, or of the lakes exist surrounded by hills in the wetter parts of the United Kingdom.

Nomen is omen they say, and do not these buildings, like so much of Camden Council's housing stock, some now demolished, borrow

THEIR NAMES FROM THE LAKE DISTRICT AND OTHER RURAL BEAUTY SPOTS: OXENHOLME, DALE HEAD, GILLFOOT, AND SILVERDALE, ESKDALE, AINSDALE, CONISTON, LANGDALE, CARTMEL, WINDERMERE, RYDAL WATER AND SO ON.

These names evoke the country in the city, just as the Dukes of Bedford evoked their countryside possessions in the city. From the ant hill, we observe the signs from nature.

ESTHER LESLIE LIVES IN SOMERS TOWN AND IS PROFESSOR OF POLITICAL AESTHETICS AT BIRKBECK COLLEGE

SHANA, PUBLIC SECTOR WORKER, DRUMMOND ST.

"I grew up in Somers Town. I loved my primary school St. Mary's - it helped set me up for the future. My dad took a real interest and I ended up going to university, which in those days was rare for a Bangladeshi girl, but my dad really supported me to do so.

I remember having fun with my friends, riding on pavements on my bike, and going to mosque after school. My mum learnt to sew at the local Hopscotch centre and she passed those skills onto me. I now work in the local area in the public sector. I loved growing up here, but I guess it was fairly rough with gangs. It has changed now."

Photo by Andy Commons

ANDY, PHOTOGRAPHER GREW UP IN PHOENIX COURT

"I grew up here with my single mum in Phoenix Court. We had great parties. At 17 I moved out and lived with my dad. A lot used to happen here between Mayford, the Cock Tavern, Chalton Street. Not a gang mentality, it's just you hung around with kids from your estate or the one next to it, just because you grew up with them and they were your mates.
I'm mixed race so wasn't that usual.
I don't know if it really was gangs, you know. Just kids hanging out."

EDIL, YOUTH CLUB, 'MELANIN-CHOLY'

"This represents my childhood for what it was – raw, urban and in the heart of one of the busiest cities in the world. I find that my childhood was one that, in the moment, couldn't be enjoyed and yet as a memory, I feel nostalgic in the places in which I made my most precious memories. Growing up, I deeply struggled with my identity as a young black woman, surrounded by masculinity and forced into feminine expectations – my photos represent me, finding the beauty in places where originally, I couldn't find happiness. My skin is ebony, my memories are filled with melancholy – my art, is melanin-choly."

Photo by Edil Saeed

OSSULSTON ESTATE, TANIA, COMMUNITY WORKER, WRITER

"I live in Levita House and work locally. I moved here from Queen's Square to escape domestic violence only to find that one of the flats had been vacated following a death as a result of domestic violence.

I am a single mother to Dontae who I home schooled to make sure his education was successful. I was thinking of what happens to young black men in London."

OSSULSTON ESTATE, DONTAE, SIXTH FORMER AND MUSICIAN

"I play trumpet and am doing physics and music at 'A' Level at college currently."

OSSULSTON ESTATE, ABDUL AND EMMANUEL, FOOTBALL CLUB

"We live in Levita House and set up the football club Camden United FC, to keep youth off the streets. We play in Regent's Park. I was born here, but my family's from Somalia and Emmanuel - his is from Ghana - he was born in UCH hospital.
Our favourite team is Chelsea - after Camden United FC."

Photos by Andy Commons

DISINTEGRATION

"I think there was a little window in history of the human race when someone in charge believed that ordinary working people like us should be provided with somwhere beautiful to live. It was brief and fleeting."

Quoted by Lynsey Hanley in 'Estates: An Intimate History' 2017

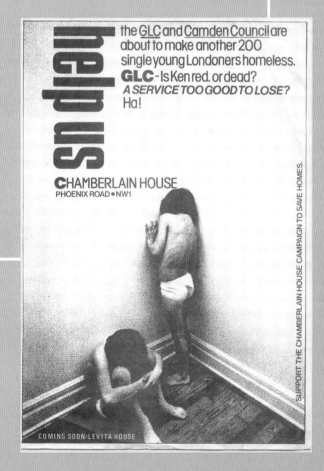

DIRECT LABOUR

BUILDING SOMERS TOWN

BY LINDA CLARKE

"IT'S MUCH BETTER TO HAVE A DIRECT LABOUR FORCE...I'VE BEEN ON THE COUNCIL SINCE 1964, WHEN WORKERS WERE ACCOUNTABLE, THEY WERE TRAINED TO BE FIRST-CLASS TRADESPEOPLE...I AM APPALLED BY SOME OF THE WORK WE SEE TODAY."

Commenting on complaints about repairs in 2016, Councillor Roger Robinson pointed out the poor quality of outsourcing by the council to the private sector.

Today many will be unaware of the important role the building departments of local authorities, known as Direct Labour Organisations or DLOs, have played and can continue to play in building and repairing council housing, especially in Somers Town. Two exemplary schemes: the Churchway Estate and the Goldington Street Estate were in Somers Town: Cecil Rhodes House and The Chenies.

FROM CROWDED TENEMENTS TO EXEMPLARY SOCIAL HOUSING PRE WW1

By the 1880s, the very vulnerability of Somers Town and its inhabitants had laid it open to incursions by the railway companies, in particular the Great Northern and Midland Railways. Evictions to make way for Kings Cross and then St. Pancras Stations only added to the crowded nature of the town.

It was therefore no surprise that Charles Booth, in his 1889 survey of the lives and occupations of the working classes in late nineteenth century London, identified many of the streets, especially around Churchway and Chalton Street, as representing some of the worst, most unhealthy housing in London. These areas were, therefore, rife for clearance and development by London County Council (LCC) under the 1890 Housing of the Working Classes Act.

The Churchway Estate, the second council house scheme in the country under the Act, was for the time exemplary, with its rubbish chutes and fine brickwork. First proposed in 1889, it was intended to house 580, with 232 on the eastern side of Churchway and 348 on the western side, though those displaced numbered 1,086.

In the end though, under the Churchway Scheme Act of 1897, the three buildings – Wellesley, Somerset and Seymour – were designed to house

850. Soon the land and buildings were being compulsory purchased by the [1]London Council Council (LCC) and by 1899 the Secretary of State had given permission for the scheme to go ahead.

Most significantly the LCC's own Works Department was commissioned to build first Wellesley Buildings, with 80 tenements, and then, in 1900, both Somerset Buildings, with 40 tenements, and Seymour Buildings, with 60. It is a testament to the Works Department that Wellesley Buildings was completed and let by May 1901, followed by Seymour Buildings in July 1902 and Somerset Buildings in August 1902 (Stilwell, 2015). It is also a testament to the quality of construction that all the buildings still stand today, though they required modernisation by the LCC in 1961.

Churchway, therefore, represents not just one of the earliest council house schemes in Britain, but one of the first to have been constructed by a DLO, in the form of the LCC Works Department. This was a time when the main function of local authorities was to act as rate-collecting agencies for paying the accounts of private contractors who were employed for all work.

Underlying the establishment of the LCC Works Department in 1893 lay a number of important conditions, the first being the poor state of housing and the second proven collusion, 'ringing of contracts' and scamped work by contractors, in particular in relation to public building work for the Metropolitan Board of Works, the predecessor of the LCC.

A third condition was the changing political environment, as local authorities were reorganized in order to provide better services and the 'Progressives' gained control of the new LCC, defeating the 'Moderates' who were more representative of the interests of local contractors and private companies.

A fourth condition was the emerging strength of the trade unions, following the mass strikes of 1888 and 1889 and the organisation of those classed as 'labourers', within the labour movement, especially through the successes of the 'Fair Wages Movement' in fighting for improved trade union conditions and for the payment of 'fair' wages agreed within any particular locality. And a final condition was the growing unemployment of the 1880s

Somerset and Seymour Buildings in 1989

and 1890s and the ineffective and temporary nature of public relief works intended to alleviate this (See Clarke 1979; Direct Labour Collective 1978).

DLOs marked a major new development in the role of local authorities. As John Burns, Progressive MP for Battersea, claimed:

The establishment of a Works Department by the Council was inevitable. It was forced on us by the contractors themselves... their withdrawing of tenders and their systematic cornering of the Council. The new Department has completely revolutionized the old corrupt order of things. It has made the Council independent in its public works. (Burns 1898)

The responsibilities of the local authorities of the time for a large range of services, including electricity, gas and transport, were reflected in the early activities of the LCC Works Department, which made all school furniture and carried out building work from a power station to new housing – including Chertsey House on the Boundary Street Estate, the first council house scheme in Britain. To support this activity, the LCC set up a variety of workshops and even founded its own brickworks. The LCC's lead was soon followed by Battersea in 1894, which carried out all its own building work, and West Ham in 1896 (Bradford Trades Council 1904).

Central to the Progressive vision was the provision of good quality and affordably priced housing, with the DLOs as a service rather than operating as an enterprise. It was seen as acting as a check on contractors and as non-profit making.

Factors such as long term maintenance cost savings were also taken into account when justifying costs and, if outside tenders were lower than direct labour estimates, this might be taken as an indication of scamped work and poor wages and conditions. Any department of the authority requiring work thus estimated the cost of this and, if the DLO accepted this estimate, then it carried out the work; if not, the work was put out to tender. Unlike other municipal activities, such as electricity and gas, the local authority was not actually selling a product, so building enterprise principles were not seen as applicable. The Churchway Estate can, therefore, be seen as an important monument to early council housing in Britain and to municipal socialism.

ST. PANCRAS BUILDS ITS OWN COUNCIL HOUSING POST WWII

Again, immediately after the second world war, Somers Town provides us with an exemplary council house scheme built by direct labour, this time by St. Pancras DLO. In February 1947, at a time when 100,000 building workers were unemployed and private contractors were not tendering at reasonable prices,

St. Pancras Council decided to set up its own DLO. This had an advisory committee of building trade unionists and its first major scheme was the construction of Cecil Rhodes House and the Chenies facing the old St. Pancras Church - particularly noted for generous space standards. This was in the context of a campaign for DLOs led by the National Federation of Building Trade Operatives and the

London Trades Council and which claimed:

Private enterprise cannot build houses to let because they do not make money that way. Private enterprise makes profit out of houses only when it builds houses to sell... the only instrument able to build houses to let in great numbers is the local authority.

The naming of the Cecil Rhodes House refers back to the historic significance of the Rhodes family to Somers Town, which was formerly Brill Farm, farmed by Thomas Rhodes, 'cowkeeper', grandfather of Cecil Rhodes and for many years Overseer and Director of the Poor in the parish of St. Pancras, whose father had in turn been a member of the Workhouse Committee and Trustee of the New (Euston) Road – built in the 1750s. And the Chenies refers to the importance of local landowner, the Duke of Bedford, also titled Baron Russell, of Chenies.

Goldington Street Estate

By 1959, when the population of St. Pancras was 130,000, the DLO employed 440 men, of whom 240 were employed on maintenance, 130 on conversions and 70 on new building (Layton 1961). By that time the DLO carried out virtually all maintenance at a cost £160,000 per year, whilst new work, at about £300,000 per year, was won by competitive tendering. John Dowling, who lived on the Estate and was a shop steward in the DLO, described in an interview how St. Pancras DLO also set up its own training scheme and encouraged other London DLOs to do the same:

WE SENT A CIRCULAR TO ALL LONDON AUTHORITIES ASKING THEM IF THEY COULD GIVE US THE FIGURES IN RELATION TO THE NUMBER OF APPRENTICES THEY EMPLOYED. AND IF NOT, WERE THEY PREPARED TO TAKE ON THE COMMITMENT... AND I MADE SURE THAT OUR DEPARTMENT CAME IN ON THAT PARTICULAR QUESTION ...AND THE NEXT THING WE HAD A FAIRLY ELABORATE TRAINING ESTABLISHMENT SET UP BY THE COUNCIL... THE POINT WAS APPRENTICESHIPS HAD BEEN SADLY LACKING IN LONDON AUTHORITIES AT THAT PARTICULAR TIME. WE STARTED THE BALL ROLLING AND IT'S NOW A COMMON FEATURE ON ALL LOCAL AUTHORITIES.

By 1978, what had become Camden DLO employed 920 people and had a turnover of £9.5m (Turner 1978). It was

noted for its pioneering employment of women, including the first qualified plumber and its fight for equal pay and against the use of 'lump' labour.

However, in 1981, after the Thatcher government imposed a moratorium on all council house building, and in the midst of recession 650 building workers were made redundant.
In 1987, the workforce was

halved again and reduced to only 70 by the end of the decade.

Photos: Camden DLO in the 1970s, including a female plumber and trainee carpenter.

Since that time, following the severe attacks on both council housing and on direct labour in the Thatcher era, many DLOs have disappeared and with them the understanding that there are alternatives to the current organisation of the construction sector. In hindsight, we can see that the departments were undermined by a number of factors, not just directly related to government enthusiasm for speculative building.

The bonus system, used as a means to attract labour into the DLOs, became a noose, hampering improvements in productivity and bearing no relation to collectively agreed rates. The strictly trade-based division of labour, evident too in apprenticeships, was a severe restraint when so many new occupations were becoming important and far broader occupational profiles were often required to meet the needs of tenants.

And, finally, the restrictions placed on the local authorities themselves were a handicap when so much would have been gained through working and sharing with other authorities.

None of these undermining factors mean that DLOs cannot take on a new life and provide the means to alleviate today's severe housing shortages, the lack of training for young people today, particularly in low energy construction, and the exclusive practices of the private sector with regard to the employment of women and those from black and Asian minority ethnic groups, and the blacklisting of trade unionists.

PROFESSOR LINDA CLARKE WROTE 'BUILDING CAPITALISM' AND HELPED SET UP THE SOMERS TOWN HISTORY WORKSHOP GROUP IN THE 1970S

Booth, C. (1889) Life and Labour of the People, Vol. I and (1891) Vol. II

Bradford Trades Council (1904) London, Battersea and West Ham Municipal Works Departments, official trade unionist report, Battersea Local History Library

Burns J (1898) London 6 January, p. 3

Clarke L (1992), Building Capitalism: historical change and the labour process in the production of the built environment, London: Routledge

Clarke L (1979), 'Direct Labour: 'goodbye to contractors'', chapter 9 in eds. Craig G., Mayo M., and Sharman N., Jobs and Community Action, Henley-on-Thames, Routledge and Kegan Paul,

Direct Labour Collective (1978), Building with Direct Labour: local authority building and the crisis in the construction industry, London: Conference of Socialist Economists8

Layton E. (1961) Building by Local Authorities, London: George, Allen and Unwin

Stilwell M. (2015, Housing the Workers: Early London County Council Housing: 1889-1914, Part 3, 19 – Churchway, St. Pancras

Turner P. (1978) Building Works and Services, London Borough of Camden report

WOLFGANG, CHAMBERLAIN HOUSE EX-SECRETARY, OSSULSTON TENANTS & RESIDENTS ASSOCIATION

"I moved into Chamberlain House in 1986, with my partner who was pregnant. There was a real mix of races andcouples expecting kids - the word was the council would house them before babies were born so they could be put into 1 bed flats, as 2 bed and larger flats were really hard to get. The estate had a functioning TRA when I arrived but I think at first my only contact was booking the hall (in the ground floor of Chamberlain House) for my daughter's birthday party - and it was great to have a nice big space with a kitchen and toilets to use, right on our doorstep.
The first person I remember was Mary, an Irish woman probably in her forties then (I was 25 or 26 when I moved in) who lived in the end flat on the first floor (directly above the hall). She seemed solid, and caring, and was known to lots of people. I don't know when I first went to meetings but I can remember a few characters. There was a writer - a burly giant with a big brown beard and a big brown actor's voice - and another man who had clearly done years and years of often thankless service, and wasn't hiding it either. I'm sure I started going partly to help put forward my socialist views but I could see it was a worthwhile thing to do.

I became secretary for a couple of years but I can't say I remember achieving much positive. There was an ongoing campaign for planting and getting the cars out of Chamberlain that I think Mary had started, and then there were security improvements offered by the council which were part of the consultation. I argued against blocking off our passage which allowed us to get through to the playground, and for a while we had a gate which could be opened either daytimes, or later I think with a residents key. It looks pretty closed now. One thing I did get personally involved in was a bid to get government funding into the area to improve community facilities. This was coordinated by a community worker linked to the Hampden Centre (now Somers Town Community Association) on Ossulston Street, and I did architectural drawings and specifications for a scheme to provide a modern kitchen that could be used to teach cooking as well as service functions, proper accessible loos, a stage with a changing area, and a play terrace facing the sun, with full height doors and a canopy. We didn't get the money sadly."

WOLFGANG, A PRACTISING ARCHITECT OF SOCIAL AND AFFORDABLE HOMES, INCL. THE GLC

HANNAH, EX-CHAMBERLAIN HOUSE

"Sandwiched between Euston and King's Cross stations, Somers Town felt like a village accidentally planted in the centre of London. My parents moved into Chamberlain House, an elegant white block with a red roof, months before I was born in 1986. I was one of the last babies on the maternity ward born at Middlesex hospital - and came back to my first home, a flat on the third floor.

I grew up scurrying alongside my dad - long-legged and often whistling - through the walkways of local estates, as he delivered anti-racist leaflets, the socialist newspaper and 'good mornings' to everyone we met. After my parents split up and my mum moved to Camden, I lived at Chamberlain half the time and was half-insider, half-outsider to estate life. Nevertheless, I felt welcomed by the local shopkeepers who knew my name and the kids on our block.

The courtyard was perfect for playing - and for testing our nascent scamming skills. Once, we went door-to-door collecting money for a fictional sponsored silence.

We lied that we were taking the challenge for charity at school but instead spent all the loose change on penny sweets at the newsagents. Another time, we learnt how to break into a car with a lolly stick and sat in the driver's seat, wheeling it around the courtyard.

When the council put in blue doors and an intercom system, there was a moment of panic because we didn't yet carry our own keys.

But we quickly solved it when we learnt the code used by firemen to get in and out. I recently returned to Somers Town to walk around alongside my dad once again - me much taller, him a little shorter - and thought about how we adapted to those doors so our community could continue.

Money has poured into King's Cross, transforming it from a place synonymous with prostitution to a centre for some of the biggest companies in the world.

Photos Diana Foster 2019

Yet Somers Town felt surprisingly similar: we bumped into people we knew and met the next generation at the community centre, learning about the history of council housing.

The village might have had to shape-shift - but I was overjoyed to see its spirit survives."

HANNAH KUCHLER IS A JOURNALIST WHO NOW LIVES IN NEW YORK

JOHN CARROLL, DRUMMOND ESTATE, PHOTOGRAPHER AND CURATOR

"My family have lived here for a long time - they still do. I've always lived in Somers Town. I went to LSE and did a degree in economics. I worked in the Anchor which my sister ran, then the off-licence and now I work in the John Soane's Museum. I am standing where I took this photo of the squatters when they were being evicted from Levita House. The old goods yard wall is visible - that was demolished for the Francis Crick construction. "

Photo by Diana Foster (2016)

THE CARROLL FAMILY, EDITH NEVILLE COTTAGES

The Carroll family outside their new home in the St. Pancras Housing Society promotional shot in the 1950s with Joyce Carroll (back row), Linda McCann, Danny Carroll, George McCann in the pram and others.
In the window is a poster for Labour MP Lena Jaeger.

Photo St. Pancras Collection
Courtesy of Camden Local Studies and Archives

MARY, EDITH NEVILLE COTTAGES, RETIRED NURSERY NURSE

"I came here from Scotland and have been here for 30 years - an incomer!

I live here with my daughter and the dog. I campaign against HS2 and we set up a newsletter so the older pople know what is going on. These cottages are up for demolition if HS2 goes ahead."

Photo by Diana Foster

SQUATTING AS A MOVEMENT

Squatting in Somers Town is a sensitive subject – as is any topic that relates to housing, who gets what house, who pays what, who has the rights to what and where. Some of the history of squatting in Somers Town is within living memory – and still rankles. There were two main periods of squatting in Somers Town – the 1970s and the 1980s. I have never squatted in Somers Town.

I tried to squat in East Berlin in 1989, when thousands of people abandoned their homes in the collapsing state of the GDR to make a life in the West – but I did not have the skills to make a dilapidated dwelling liveable. I too fled to the West. This research comes from browsings in the Camden Local Studies Archive, the Bishopsgate Institute, research in newspaper and picture archives online, including the materials gathered by History Pin, and from conversations with participants in squats in both the 1970s and 1980s.

The squats in Somers Town, especially those from the 1980s, have attracted little attention subsequently and leave few archival traces. It is not like the battles for Tolmers Square, which produced a book and a film, or the Huntley Street Commune or 144 Piccadilly – which were more notorious squats. It is hard to reconstruct the tissue of experiences. This is, then, just a small stab at it.

Squatting was a significant phenomenon in the late 1960s. It took off in outer London areas, such as Redbridge, where activists, most notably Ron Bailey, helped homeless families into empty houses. Bailey had been working through the 1960s with homeless families. Councils had a duty to house them, but they fulfilled this duty by placing them in squalid hostels, sometimes separating men from women and children.

Activists began to squat derelict or abandoned buildings, citing a law, devised by the Barons in 1381, against 'forcible entry'. This meant that no one could break into a property and evict who was occupying it without first obtaining a court order and naming the occupant. In Redbridge the council had bought up and boarded up a thousand houses. They were waiting for a time to pull them down and redevelop the area.

Activists had installed homeless families in empty council owned properties. That was the start of a new squatting campaign in London, led by the Family Squatting Advisory Service. Homes were occupied as short life housing on a 'no rent, no repairs' basis. Rates, water and electricity bills were paid. The council in Essex saw reason in this.

But some councils did not cooperate and so direct action was taken.[1] Need was huge. In a 1971 census:

THERE WERE 12 000 HOMELESS FAMILIES, 100 0000 FAMILIES ON THE WAITING LIST FOR A HOME IN 13 LONDON BOROUGHS. AT THE SAME TIME, THERE WERE 100 000 EMPTY HOMES IN GREATER LONDON.

Georgian and Neo-Georgian terraces stood derelict in Camden in the 1960s. Developers had bought up chunks in order to demolish them. Private estates were planned. Some houses were compulsorily purchased as part of schemes to widen roads.

Camden Council had plans for new social housing. Camden Council bought the writer Doris Lessing, for example, out of her home in 60 Charrington Street, under a compulsory purchase order. But money was not to be found for the large developments and things just festered. The houses in North Somers Town, on Charrington Street, Penryn Street and Medburn Street stood empty and decaying.

SQUATTING NORTH

Of 22,500 council-owned dwellings in Camden, 1003 were unoccupied, some awaiting demolition, the majority in need of modernisation and renovation. Many were old stock lacking inside toilets or bathrooms.

Camden Council planned to start renovating properties in and around Charrington Street in 1968. By 1973, only 3 had been partially renovated. An economic slump had hit and it was unclear if these old buildings should be pulled down and rebuilt or brought up to scratch. Squatters were already occupying the buildings. In August 1972, squatters occupied a derelict corner shop and claimed squatters' rights.

The squatters' community built up from there with around 260 people in several houses. These houses were in a decent enough condition to live in. Squatters made their improvements. They knocked down interior walls and installed home-made showers.

SQUATTING

IN SOCIAL HOUSING

BY ESTHER LESLIE

1   For more details, see Ron Bailey, The Squatters, Harmondsworth, Penguin, 1973.

The absence of interior walls allowed for a more communal mode of living. The squatters were mainly single people, unable to gain housing from the council and squeezed out of tenancies in London by high private rents. Many were students.

It is possible to build up a picture of life here. The BBC made a film which was broadcast in on 7 November 1973. It is titled Somers Town Squatters. The Radio Times described its contents:

THE FIRST OF A SERIES OF SIX PROGRAMMES ABOUT SIX DIFFERENT GROUPS OF YOUNG PEOPLE WHO ARE DISSATISFIED WITH THE SOCIETY IN WHICH THEY LIVE AND ARE TRYING, IN THEIR OWN WAY, TO CHANGE IT. THE SOMERS TOWN SQUATTERS ARE A LOOSELY KNIT GROUP OF 200-300 YOUNG PEOPLE WHO HAVE TAKEN OVER A BLOCK OF OLD HOUSES IN LONDON AND MADE THEIR HOMES THERE.[2]

Other sources give an indication of what life was like in the communes and flats. There was a newsletter, Community News and Culture[3]. Its editorial address was split between 24 Charrington Street and the Great Joint Happiness Commune at 54 Charrington Street. The latter was the name of the renamed grocers, which functioned as a community trading centre, selling health foods, as well as dispensing ideas and legal advice.

The newsletter came to be printed by the Islington Free Press by offset litho – which accounted for what appeared to be a price rise to 5p for ongoing issues. Inside one issue was a critical review of The Squatters by Ron Bailey. This is a telling article because it reveals differences between the squatters' movement of 1968 and this one in the early 1970s.

The review gave praise where it was due:

'WE NEED FEAR NO MORE COUNCIL "HEAVIES"; WE CAN MAKE DEMANDS ON THE COUNCIL ...'

But it also noted that Bailey worked together with councils. Camden and Islington squatters, in contrast, followed the more anarchistic anti-state lead set by the London Street Commune – at 144 Piccadilly. The Somers Town newsletter characterised their stance as that of 'Communards "rejecting the work syndrome, compartmentalized conditions of straight society'. But they were practical too – engaged in organising, repairing, restoring houses. And all this occurred without 'chairmen'.

Another item dealt with in the newsletter detailed a battle between 24 and 26 Charrington St. and the London Electricity Board. The Greater London Council, the ruling body of London, had tried to stop the LEB entering and hooking up the electricity supply. The Charrington Street squatters were in the midst of a court case. They were not alone in this – squatters organisations were working to establish the principle that electricity should be supplied to anyone who was in a

house and willing to pay a deposit.

Squatters in this period were broadly organised to deal with such issues collectively. The grouping All London Squatters held a meeting at The Roebuck, Tottenham Court Road, London W1, on Sunday, 6 January 1974. The minutes record that approximately 95 people were present. It relates a success at Charrington Street, noting:

THE GLC COUNCILLORS ARE SCARED ABOUT THEIR PUBLIC IMAGE. LABOUR ARE STILL NOT SURE OF THEMSELVES, AND THEREFORE THEY ARE WILLING TO MEET US AND DISCUSS THINGS. THE GLC BACKED DOWN IN THE CASE OF CHARRINGTON STREET. WE ARE GOING TO GO AHEAD AT ALL LEVELS, BUT WE MUST START IMMEDIATELY[4].

This incident provides a window into tensions between the GLC, councils, utilities and services. Another example is Camden Council's banning of squatters from using library facilities in 1973. The council issued a directive instructing staff that squatters were not classed as 'residents' and were therefore not entitled to borrow books. Attempts were made to prevent squatters obtaining advice from council-aided advice groups. Direct action and organised pressure got some of these things revoked.

The squatters Somers Town, or Summerstown, newsletter, as it was titled, announced a Spring Festival in Charrington Street with fertility rites and the establishment of the Somers Town Claimants Union at a meeting in 9 Penryn Street. A benefit dance at the Old Hampstead Town Hall made £100 split 50/50 between GHJC and the Pasha/Peoples Promotion Collective – half of which went to a playgroup.

Elsewhere in the Summerstown newsletter there is an announcement about a march on the Ideal Homes

Photos Ray Adamson, courtesy of daughter.

2   Radio Times, Issue 2608, p. 59. 1 November 1973.
3   One copy exists in the Bishopsgate Institute Archive of Squatting materials.
4   Squatting Archive – ALS Meeting (6 Jan 74). http://www.wussu.com

exhibition. This event, promoted by the Daily Mail newspaper, was an outrage, they noted, in a situation where 50 000 London people had no home at all, let alone an ideal one.

Terry Collins, one of the Charrington Street squatters, a teacher living alongside 'junior doctors and lawyers, artists, mechanics and musicians, as well as a few who fit the image of vagrants', provided vivid memories of this: Here just some extracts from his online reminiscences.

"'Housing For All' was our slogan and Self-Help our credo; we improved the houses we were occupying because they were our homes, and we didn't see ourselves as consumers needing the latest gadget because we were only concerned with our needs. The annual Ideal Home Exhibition was the antithesis of our core idealism.

We knew that parading with handheld placards outside the venue, the giant Earls Court Arena, would only antagonise the attendees and exhibitors, and could also lead to our arrests. That the exhibition had been sponsored since 1908 by a right wing daily newspaper, the Daily Mail, simplified matters.

THE DAILY HERNIA WAS BORN. WE SAW IT AS AN ALTERNATIVE PRIVATE EYE, THE UK'S SEMI-SATIRICAL FORTNIGHTLY MAGAZINE WITH A SERIOUS SIDE. WE SOUGHT CONTRIBUTIONS FROM WHOEVER WANTED TO JOIN US: OUR HOROSCOPES REFLECTED OUR COLLECTIVE NINE ASTROLOGICAL SIGNS, THERE WERE SMALL ADS AND A BIG HEADLINE EXTOLLING THE SOUVENIR EDITION OF THE DAILY HERNIA'S IDEAL HUT EXHIBITION. THERE WERE I SUSPECT (BUT FORGET) SERIOUS ARTICLES ON HOMELESSNESS, THE LEGAL RIGHTS OF SQUATTERS – WHICH DATED BACK TO THE 14TH CENTURY, PLUS OTHER RELEVANT MATTERS.

What I do recall is the theatrical nature of our demo. We got hold of some long white lab coats, stencilled Daily Hernia on the back, took our stack of 'newspapers', made our way across London and then looked to get in without paying. The exits were the type found in cinemas: to get out you had to push a bar, the door(s) then swung shut and locked. Beside each door inside was a 'gatekeeper' who was there to prevent the likes of us getting in: we found one who was sympathetic to our cause.

Once in, we separated and wended our way along the aisles between the exhibitor stands.

"Try me and stop one," we cried out. "Get your free

issue here."
"Free?"
Yep, such is consumerism that we soon ran out of stock. We returned the following year, and for me that was significant for a conversation I had with a lady who'd travelled down from Blackpool in north-west England.
"Eh lad," she said, "I'm glad you're here. I got a copy last year and wanted another one." I would have offered her a subscription, but that would have been too consumerist."[5]

Other traces of this community can be gathered. For example, various reports relate that one morning in 1973 all but one of the 60 or so squatted houses were raided by the Bomb Squad. The police were looking for Surface to Air Missiles that could bring down jumbo jets bound for Heathrow airport. Terry Collins finds the thought that such weapons would have been harboured there absurd – many of the squatters worked and led fairly ordinary lives and were not terrorists.

Out of this experience, and the consequent anger at police heavy-handedness, an ad hoc committee was formed. There is evidence of it in a notice in the New Statesman in 1973:

DEFENCE OF CIVIL LIBERTIES MARCH ASSEMBLE 2 P.M. SATURDAY 6 OCTOBER AT CHARRINGTON ST., NW1. MARCH TO NEW SCOTLAND YARD. ORG. BY LONDON AD HOC COMMITTEE FOR THE DEFENCE OF CIVIL LIBERTIES.

The demo was proposed by Sid Rawle, whom the press dubbed King of the Hippies – he was head of the Camden Federation of Squatters. The demonstrators carried a papier mache bomb, which was confiscated by police.

Mick Brown wrote an article on the Charrington Street squatters in July 1973, titled 'Be It Ever So Humble, There's No Place Like Home', arguing that this was a political action to generate new, different forms of community for young people and different thinkers.

'PEOPLE WHO'VE NEVER HAD THE TIME OR OPPORTUNITY TO CREATE THEIR OWN ENVIRONMENT CAN NOW INFLUENCE THE WAY THEY LIVE' SAID A SQUATTER. TOOLS ARE SWAPPED AROUND. LEAD PIPING IS SWAPPED FOR NUTS AND BOLTS. CAMDEN COUNCIL LEAVES THEM ALONE. POLICE CARS PATROL THE AREA BUT WITHOUT INTERVENTION.

Several empty houses on the block had their toilets smashed and lead pipes pulled out. They were 'tinned', boarded up with corrugated iron. But they get liberated once the van has left.

---

5   See Terry Collins' reminiscences at http://jakartass.net for more on this.

'THE FEW REMAINING COUNCIL TENANTS LIVING IN THE BLOCK DON'T SEEM TO MIND EITHER. THEY REALISE WE'RE UTILISING THE EMPTY PROPERTIES. THEY'VE SAID THEY FEEL SAFER WITH US HERE THAN WITH HOMES EMPTY, ANYWAY, BECAUSE OF THE VANDALS WHO WERE ALWAYS BREAKING INTO PLACES'.[6]

The implication is that there is more community in these squatted houses than in the new tower blocks that were springing up in the vicinity and elsewhere. Brown's article mentions the presence of the council wrecker. There exists a news item on film from 1975, which shows Camden Council's wreckers in action elsewhere in the borough – though John Mills, who is interviewed in the film, states that the policy is mistaken and would not be repeated.

Brown also reveals that the average weekly income of a squatter was £7 – so while the insides of the houses might be renovated, the outsides remained dilapidated, because residents' wages were sparse.

Not everyone was poor though – a contemporaneous report in the local newspaper, the Camden Journal, mentions Aidan Quin, a mechanic operating from one of the houses in North Somers Town. He was running a massive and lucrative car repair and import business.

There are other hints of life at Charrington Street in the early 1970s floating in the strange ether of the web. Steve Andrews relates a ghost story, which gives a more negative impression of how life might be lived in the 1970s squats:[7]

"IT WAS IN LONDON IN 1972 WHEN I WAS 19 AND IN MY DECADENT HIPPIE DAYS AND IT MUST HAVE BEEN A WEEK OR SO AFTER THE FREE WINDSOR FESTIVAL. I WAS LIVING IN CARDIFF AT THE TIME BUT MET A GIRL AT THE FESTIVAL WHO WAS LIVING IN A SQUAT IN LONDON AND SHE INVITED ME THERE. BEING ATTRACTED TO THE GIRL I WENT BACK TO WHERE I LIVED TO GET A CHANGE OF CLOTHES AND A FEW THINGS AND THEN HITCHED TO LONDON WITH MY FRIEND STEVE.

The squat was in Charrington Street in Camden Town and had actually been featured in a BBC2 TV documentary called 'Annie Come Home ' but the girl I was hoping to see was Ali. I found she had apparently gone hop-picking in Kent with someone else.

THE HOUSES WERE OFTEN IN A TERRIBLE STATE AS WERE THE PEOPLE LIVING IN THEM WHO WERE MAINLY PEOPLE WITH DRUG AND ALCOHOL OR MENTAL HEALTH PROBLEMS OR ALL THREE. ONE OF THE SQUATTERS WAS AN EX-HELL'S ANGEL CALLED BIG MICK. I MENTION HIM NOW BECAUSE HE COMES INTO THE STORY LATER ON.

Mick was a very big guy and taller than me and looked tough. He had tattoos and stubble and muscly arms and if there was any trouble he was someone who was called on to sort it out. Steve and I were told the house we were in was haunted and a few days later we were to find out this was true. We had gone to the local pub and afterwards went back to the squat but on the way in through the door both of us felt very cold even though it was a hot end of summer's night. We made our way upstairs though and found the floor we were staying on.

The houses were old terraces and basically people just dossed down on the floor in sleeping bags. There were always several people sleeping in the same room. There was no electricity and people used torches or candles.

The place was really squalid and people threw rubbish out the window into the stinking pile of garbage below. Floorboards and doors were missing and had been used as firewood. The basic rules of possession were if you valued something you kept it with you otherwise it was up for grabs."

The ghostly experience occurs: a luminous green glow emanating from the neck of the Hell's Angel and a weird experience known apparently as a 'hummadruz'. This perhaps indicates something of the kind of spiritual and offbeat ideas around in the communes of the time.

Another dark story from that time concerns Robin Farquharson, who lived for some time in the squats. He certainly was one of the mentally disturbed, as well as being an extraordinary mathematician who had written about game theory.

In 1964 he was still an academic. A little later, he had

---

6   Excerpted pages in Bishopsgate Institute Archive of Squatting materials; name of magazine not evident.

7   https://wizzley.com/paranormal-experiences-in-a-haunted-london-squat/

dropped out, as is reflected in the title of his memoir Drop Out![8] He was also the founder of the Mental Patients Union, a self-organised grouping for mental health patients, which met in Charrington Street. As the MPU meeting minutes state:

Robin Farquharson offered accommodation in Charrington St.. N.W.1 for the MPU in a house that has been procured by squatting and needs a certain amount of repair. Offer accepted.[9] In April 1973, Farquharson was living in a squat in Platt Street. He was not in a good way. A fire in the house led to his death – a trial decided that the fire was the result of arson and two workers living in the squat with him were convicted of unlawful killing.

Norman Tebbit, the Member of Parliament, channelled some of the negative energy around the squats. The Hansard minutes of a Housing Committee Debate on 20 November 1973 record the following:

MR. TEBBIT, THE HON. MEMBER FOR HACKNEY, CENTRAL SAYS, 'ABSURD'. PERHAPS I SHOULD DRAW TO HIS ATTENTION A COMPLAINT MADE ABOUT THE NUMBER OF SQUATTERS IN SOMERS TOWN: FEW WERE REALLY HOMELESS AND MOST WERE MIXED-UP KIDDIES ACTING OUT THEIR MIDDLE-CLASS GUILT. COUNCIL TENANTS HAVE SUFFERED A BARRAGE OF INTENSE NOISE, MUSIC, NUDITY, FIRES, VERMIN AND MORE DEFIANT BEHAVIOUR THAN ANYONE COULD LEGALLY PUBLISH A BOOK ON. THIS WAS DESCRIBED BY THE SPEAKER CONCERNED AS 'INTENSE PROVOCATION' AND ALSO AS A 'VIOLENT STREET CONFRONTATION'.

THAT WAS NOT SAID BY SOME DIEHARD; IT WAS SAID BY A GENTLEMAN CALLED MR. KAZANTZIS, A LABOUR GLC MEMBER FROM SOMERS TOWN, WHO BELIEVED THAT THOSE SQUATTERS WERE NOT HOMELESS AT ALL BUT WERE TROUBLEMAKERS. THIS IS WHAT WILL HAPPEN ALL THE TIME IF LOCAL AUTHORITIES OPEN UP THEIR HOUSING LISTS TO ALL COMERS.'[10]

Tebbit was referring to Alexander or Alec John Kazantzis, of the Labour Party, who stood for election to the GLC in 1973 for Camden, Holborn and St. Pancras South. He won with 7,437 votes, 60% of the total cast. One of his opponents was P. Goulstone who garnered just 60 votes. Goulstone stood for the Great Joint Happiness Homes for All (GJHH) party, emanating out of Charrington Street. As Terry Collins recalls:

"WE EMPHASISED THE NEED FOR 'HOUSING FOR ALL'. WE WERE TEACHERS, DOCTORS, MUSICIANS AND DERELICTS TRYING TO GET ALONG; WE PROPOSED THE GLC HARD-TO-LET POLICY AND WERE 'OFFERED' ALTERNATIVE EMPTY GLC PROPERTIES WHEN IT CAME TIME TO MOVE.'

TOLMERS SQUARE / 1970s

The squatters claimed some victories, small ones that fitted their smaller-scale, practical politics, as suggested in an email from former squatter Terry Collins on 21 September 2016, 'our politics were not one of confrontation. Which is to say that the brother of Jeremy Corbyn, Piers, preferred to live behind barricades in Elgin Avenue (?), where as we were 'creative', satirical even, in making our 'protests' about leaving habitable properties empty when all we wanted to do was live decent lives, in tune with our neighbours. That we were able to negotiate with the GLC for new premises to move into when they were ready to renovate the ones we were occupying - yes, we were given a licence to remain - suggests that we all benefitted'.

Camden Council allowed squatters to stay in short-life property:

'PROVIDING THEY ARE NOT A NUISANCE TO THEIR NEIGHBOURS AND ARE NOT PREVENTING THE COUNCIL [FROM] HOUSING PEOPLE OFF THE WAITING LIST'.

It took 'immediate legal action to get rid of squatters in anything but its short-life properties'. It smashed up empty properties to make squatting impossible and seldom offered rehousing to people it evicted. In a press statement of 19 March 1975, it declared: 'Camden takes the view that short-life houses are better in use than left empty.' [11] The squats in Charrington Street were moved on eventually. Camden sent in the wreckers and the builders. The houses accommodated a variety of tenants and owners in the subsequent years. Today, 9 Penryn St. sells for well over a million or a rent of more than £4000 a month.

The Squatting movement retreated as the 1970s went on. The need for homes did not disappear though. It just became harder to squat. The idea of the holidaymaker who returns to a squatted home became a staple of TV sit coms. Squatters were demonised. New legislation closed loopholes. The Criminal Law Act of 1977 repealed the forcible entry acts. Owners could eventually get an eviction order and bailiffs could break into empty houses and move possessions. To avoid eviction, squatters needed to have someone in permanent possession of the building.

1980S: SQUATTING SOUTH

Perusal of the newspapers, the Camden Journal and the St. Pancras Chronicle in the early 1908s, reveals story after story about tenants' dissatisfaction with the state of their homes on the Ossulston Estate. In the Camden Journal of 17 October 1980, drainage problems are reported at Levita House. Somers Town feels neglected and undermined. Wellesley House is under threat because"it is in the path of new bus lanes. Chalton Street is losing its small shops and becoming derelict. In Walker House, half the flats are empty and boarded up.

8   Robin Farquharson, Drop Out!, Anthony Blond, London, 1968.

9 Cited at Mental Health and Survivors' Movements and Contexts, http://studymore.org.uk/ mpu

10   Findable at http://hansard.mill¬banksystems.com/commons/1973/ nov/20/london-public-servic¬es#S5CV0864P0_19731120_ HOC_333

11   Roof, 1984

On 23 October 1981, the St. Pancras Chronicle reports that the go ahead has been given by the GLC to modernise Levita and Walker House, but the works do not start. In the Camden New Journal, on 30 September 1982, there is a report of 40 angry residents marching to the Town Hall with a jar of cockroaches gathered from the Ossulston Estate. The homes there were in a poor state and many were uninhabited. Squatters moved in to the blocks. I spoke to one, Daniel, who had vivid memories of the time. He was training to be a hairdresser with Vidal Sassoon and wanted to be in London amongst punks and artists. He recalled the state of the kitchens in Chamberlain House: there was no bathroom but there was a bath and it doubled up as a kitchen cutting surface once a lid was put over it.

The squats lasted a couple of years, in the midst of heavy security guards sent down from the British Library construction site.[12] The inevitable eviction orders came, once the funds for renovation were received in 1984 from the GLC. But the battle to remove squatters was protracted. City Limits magazine, from the week of 8-14 June 1984, has the following report:

'200 squatters in Somers Town have been told to get out or face eviction. Mostly young and single. Squatters say there are nearly 2000 empty properties in the borough. The flats in Chamberlain house are not amongst those considered fit for habitation. But as Jeremy (Hardy), a stand up comic, points out: 'We don't have any emotional clout like people with kids, so they just push us around. But we've been here a year and stopped this place falling apart'.

An interview with squatters Una Sapietis and Catherine Campbell in the St. Pancras Chronicle, on 15 June 1984, makes a similar point. The squatters were single homeless people and there was no provision otherwise. They held on to their homes. Where would they go? Jane Penton, a squatter in the area, reports that:

WE MOBILISED AS A POLITICAL HOMELESS GROUP AND SOLICITED CAMDEN COUNCIL TO ALLOW US TO FORM CO-OPS AND RENOVATE OTHER LESS DESIRABLE EMPTY BUILDINGS IN THE BOROUGH. OUR FRIENDS IN ISLINGTON HAD THESE ARRANGEMENTS, AND HAD MUCH BETTER HOUSING SECURITY.

[13] The squatters pleaded their case with Labour leader, Neil Kinnock, when he visited shiny new Tolmers Square, where a squat had been cleared. They took direct action to stay – or be rehoused. The St. Pancras Chronicle, on 22 June 1984, reports on how squatters threw petrol bombs at police in defiance of a mass eviction. Riot police moved

in on a Wednesday night. Squatters set fire to two flats and heaped furniture in the courtyard.

On 15 July 1984, newspapers report that eviction is delayed. The tensions mount and a battle of words is played out in the local press. The £1 million renovation programme was not ready to begin. The Ossulston Estate TA argued that Chamberlain House, which was almost completely occupied by squatters, had been devastated.

The original tenants of Chamberlain House had been rehoused but wanted to return when flats were ready. Jeremy Hardy, the tenants' rep, dismissed the claims that squatters had acted destructively. Eviction notes were sent out to squatters in Levita House on 5 February 1985, including to the 48 squatters and caravan dwellers in the courtyard. By mistake they were sent to all tenants, causing panic. A TV clip from Thames News in April 1985 shows squatters in temporary accommodation after being removed from Levita House. In May 1985, there was a huge fire in Chamberlain House, and 70 short-life tenants and squatters were made homeless. Jane Penton recalls a fiery event at Chamberlain House:

THERE WERE SEVERAL ABANDONED CARS IN THE COURTYARD WHICH WERE SET ON FIRE. WE HAD STAIRWELLS AND BALCONIES FACING THE COURTYARD SO COULD MERRILY (AND SAFELY) OFFER TORPEDOES OF UNWANTED FURNITURE, TV'S ETC TO THE BURNING MAYHEM. THE FIRE-BRIGADE CAME AND DOUSED THINGS AT REGULAR INTERVALS WITHOUT ANY MISSILES BEING FIRED... BUT AS SOON AS THEY LEFT TO GENERAL CHEERS AND APPLAUD, THE BURNING WOULD BEGIN AGAIN.[14]

In 1985, the Advisory Service for Squatters estimated that there were 30-35 000 squatters in London, more than in the 1970s, and equal to the squatting boom of 1946. The Board and Lodging regulation was reintroduced in 23 November 1985, meaning that people under the age of 26 could only get rent-paying benefits for 8 weeks, despite having taken up the aforementioned Norman Tebbit's advice and 'got on their bikes' to find work elsewhere in the country. The squatters left eventually. The money came in for renovations. The St. Pancras Chronicle, on 9 March 1992, reports, for example, on the reopening of Levita House with West Hampstead Housing carrying out the works.

ESTHER LESLIE, PROFESSOR OF POLITICAL AESTHETICS AND LIVES IN SOMERS TOWN

Photos by Ray Adamson, courtesy of his daughter Zoe

---

12 History Pin interview
13 History Pin interview
14 History Pin interview

KEN, RETIRED COMMUNITY WORKER, ST MARTIN'S HOUSE

"I came here in 1985 and was squatting in Levita House then I got a flat here. I worked at an advice centre, run by Voluntary Action Camden - we used to help set up Tenants Associations and give advice on housing, emploryment and immigration. We had a Bengali-speaking community worker, too, as the number of Bengalis increased. In the '80s unemployment was high, the Tory government made cuts, the squatting got out of hand.Somers Town had a lot of poverty - it didn't show, but only when working that I realised. You don't really see social problems unless you work in it. People don't tend to talk about their problems. You can be well dressed and poor as a church mouse.
I'd always get to work to a crowd outside wanting advice.

There was a huge problem with homelessness and Somers Town became a focal point for squatting. Levita house was very run down and the council was used for temporary housing for the homeless. You had to have some problem to be a priority to get on the housing list, so we spent a lot of time trying to get people through the housing regulations. Most people working in the council were sympathetic.

I wonder what has happened to all the people that need help that don't get it now."

Photo by John Carroll

AB, OSSULSTON ESTATE

"My family and me were evicted from a tied flat when our dad died. The job was his. Mum was at breaking point - she'd been homeless three times. So when we got the council flat, we were so happy. Later we took the right to buy - we didn't want to be homeless again."

JOHN, CARETAKER

"I worked for 30 years at the local primary school, and I loved it, unitl a new headteacher bullied me. I walked out because of the stress. Now they tell me I cannot stay in the house - they are going to knock this down for rebuilding the school and private flats -part of the Community Investment Programme. I have nowhere to go, and have only been offered hostels - but my daughter cannot stay in a hostel - or flats outside the area that are too expensive. I thought I had this for life - in the past the caretakers did have housing for life. I'm going to be evicted."

IZZY AND BARNEY THE DOG, ST. CHRISTOPHER'S FLATS

"I was homeless before I got this flat. When I moved in I didn't unpack for six months. I just slept with all my stuff in the middle of the living room.

I live here with Barney, who I rescued.. When I got him, everything changed.
I saved him and he saved me."

Photo by Andy Commons

IN CONVERSATION

WITH DAVID TOVEY ARTIST ACTIVIST

What was the biggest factor in driving this project over the past 4 years to become what it is today?

My stubbornness to be honest with you.

I GOT SO FED UP WITH PEOPLE PUTTING HOMELESS PEOPLE DOWN ALL THE TIME

and I could see how great they can be if they are given the space to share their work. This keeps driving me. When your project changes ones life then you know you are doing it right.

Can you tell us about being a representative for the homeless community yourself, do you feel your story acts as a beacon for other people struggling with homelessness?

I hope so. It is a difficult one because I feel that sometimes because I have been recognised for my work it hinders me a bit. I don't want the festival to be about me, I want it to be about

other people,

I'm just the one who puts it together.

I WANT THE FESTIVAL TO BE ABOUT THE ARTISTS, THEIR WORK AND THEIR STORIES

I see it as – I'm trying to turn my life around and if other people can get something from that, then great. I'm quite shy about it all.

How can the One Fest help others in adverse situations take the next steps in their life?

It gives people an opportunity to get their voices heard and work seen. I don't really like the word 'empower', but the Festival sort of gives people the confidence that their work is important, plus all the people who use Old Diorama or work at Regent's Place or are just passing through also

get to see the work.

So, David if you could say one line to anyone about the festival what would it be?

IT IS A PLACE TO COME AND HAVE YOUR PERCEPTIONS CHANGED. THAT IS THE WHOLE POINT.

Can you outline some of the toughest aspects of delivering the One Festival?

My health, my mental health, not being a charity, just being me – sometimes I wish I was 10 people it would make it so much easier! Also funding – and this is where Regent's Place, Old Diorama and Camden People's Theatre being on board makes all the difference, I really couldn't do this otherwise.

What is the most important factor when you're pulling together this event?

The Art. First and foremost. When you've got the art you build the festival around it. There is so much you can do with a pencil and a piece of paper, it can change lives. That is why I have the pencil drawing next to the oil painting, it is all relative. To get someone to focus on just 10 minutes drawing makes such a difference, I see it in the workshops I do – just the emotional change from being completely angry to smiling and calm.

I imagine seeing all these people come together to celebrate artforms, all created by those who have been suffering with homeless must be immeasurable. How does it make you feel seeing this all come together?

Emotional. Just even thinking about it, I never thought I'd be able to do this to be honest and now it is 4 years in a row. I started organising this year's festival back in January, 10 months of hard work so in a way it gives me relief. It also makes me feel so proud.

The thing is I'm still going through some of the same things people exhibiting are going through, so yeah, it makes me feel very proud.

Can you tell us about the artwork to be displayed and about the curation process?

A lot of it I didn't see until it arrived – SHP, I knew what was coming from them, Geraldine Crimmins – I know her work well but the international art – like from America – I didn't have a clue! The theme this year of bringing the 'Outsiders In' really helped with the curation this year.

If you weren't the organiser and was attending as a visitor, what would be your top three must-see elements of this year's festival?

Ooh... the theatre, of course the artworks and Streetwise Opera performing at the Launch Event. Also to see all the other visitors. it is the community, and to see everyone mixing, it gives such a special feel. You get all walks of life you really do –

PEOPLE IN SUITS HUGGING PEOPLE ROUGH SLEEPING

Last of all, could you give us a little glimpse into the future of the One Festival of Homeless Arts – what would you most like to achieve in the next few years?

What is great about it, although it is London based, is that it is also in Manchester and Gloucester this year. I hope to see more cities and exhibitions in the future, the festival is about everyone getting involved, so to do more would be great.

DAVID TOVEY, ARTIST, ACTIVIST, AND FOUNDING DIRECTOR OF THE ONE FESTIVAL OF HOMELESS ARTS, INITIALLY ARTIST IN RESIDENCE AT OLD DIORAMA.

October 2019
www.onefestivalofhomelessarts.com/

David Tovey at the Festival

THE STATE WE'RE IN

A TO Z

A RANDOM ALPHABET BY DONNA TURNBULL

The state we're in 100 years on from Addison: a random alphabet of stuff to read, watch and research. Part bibliography, and part statements and subjects to explore, an alphabetical perspective on the global and historical context for the current housing crisis.

D- DISPOSSESSION

Paul Sng's film shows the plight of council housing residents in the face of estate 'regeneration'.

HOUSING CRISIS

FOR SALE

E- ELEPHANT AND CASTLE

An area of London that illustrates the perfect storm of social cleansing, political self-interest and free market development. The 35% Campaign blog reflects the journey from council homes to asset building investments.

A - ASH

Architects for Social Housing website unpicks government 'regeneration' of council estates, presents alternatives, and explores a contemporary approach for a socialist architecture.

F - FAKE NEWS

Affordable housing. In truth, refers to a range of 'products' for sale or rent at below market rates. Market rates are so high 'discounted' housing is rarely affordable to those who need it. Social housing is a small % of the small affordable % of a new housing development. Social housing is rarely Council housing.

B - BENEFITS

Every year around £9 billion goes to private landlords in housing benefits.

H - HOMELESSNESS

A growth industry with big profits for private landlords. The state paid over £1 billion last year for increasing numbers of people excluded from housing to stay in temporary accommodation.

C - CREDIT

Cheap credit driving up house prices and opportunity for profit making products: Buy to Let, Let to Buy, Rent to Buy.........

G - GLOBAL FINANCE

Global investors buy up property and extract profit from inflated land values. Post gentrification, housing is an investment product, destroying the social fabric of cities and further enriching the wealthy. Frank Gerten's documentary Push illustrates some of the big picture.

I - IDEOLOGY

The way government delivers housing is led by ideology, not economics.

J - JUSTICE

www.grenfellunited.org.uk
www.justice4grenfell.org
www.grenfellactiongroup.wordpress.com

L - LAND VALUE

The high cost of land, based on aspiration of owners, rather than the reality of what can and should be done with that land (true market value), underpins the housing crisis.

K - SADIQ KHAN

Khan, Sadiq. Mayor of London. Read between the lines in the London plan and use Just Space website to understand housing policy in the capital.

M - MUNICIPAL DREAMS

John Boughton's book charting the rise and fall of council housing.

N - NEO LIBERALISM

The dominant ideology of now. Deregulation, austerity, individualism, and the survival of the fittest.

O - OUR COMMON GROUND

Land Justice Network statement advocating for the land reform needed to support environmental and social justice.

P - POLITICIANS

Registers of Interest (and voting records) reveal personal land and property interests of elected representatives.

Q - QUICKFIX & QUASI HOUSING

Shelter's blog among others describes some of the pitiful ideas trying to address government failure to supply the housing people need...... prefabs, shipping containers, 'window boxes', student style dorms.

R - RADICAL SOLUTIONS

Solutions for the Housing Supply Crisis: Duncan Bowie sets out the reforms required to address the failure of housing policies and housing supply.

S - SAVILLS

Global property agent. Produced 2017 Housing White Paper recommending Build to Rent and other housing products lucrative for developers. Their report 'Completing London's Streets' is a blueprint for council estate 'regeneration'.

T - TOWN & COUNTRY ACT

The Town and Country Planning Act of 1947 was the start of modern planning included provision for Compensation and Betterment to capture the uplift in value from land for public good. The more recent Raynsford Review suggests bringing it back in some form.

U - UPLIFT

The difference between the value of land, and the value of the same land once it is developed.

W - WHO OWNS ENGLAND?

Guy Shrubsole journeys through land ownership. From the 11th century Norman land grab (from the many for the few) to present day property portfolios.

V - VIABILITY ASSESSMENT

Developers use Economic Viability Assessments to override local planning policy and avoid building genuinely affordable housing.

Y - YOUNG PEOPLE

Some of the biggest losers in the dehumanised world of housing where by the Government's own definition at least 65% of all new housing development is unaffordable.

X - XR

Declaring climate emergency whilst pursuing greed and growth models for housing delivery.... arse and elbow.

Z - ZAPATISMO

An intuition that compels one to say 'enough' in the face of injustice. A concept for now.

ACKNOWLEDGEMENTS

With thanks to all who contributed help, anecdotes and photographs:

Zoe Adamson
Rose Alexander
Tudor Allen
John Carroll, Joyce and Pat Carroll
Stephen Denholm
Malcolm Holmes
Ken Jones
John Kent
Paul Lowne
Joyce Mansur
Mimi Romilly
George Sharp
Nelly Sharp
Alan Stephens
David Tovey
Danny Twyman
Mary Wood

All work is copyright of the orginal authors.

Copyright © 2019 Authors

Professor Linda Clarke
John Cowley
Carrie de Silva
Diana Foster
Joe Kerr
Hannah Küchler
Wolfgang Küchler
Deborah Lavin
Professor Esther Leslie
Jackie Lewis
Michael Parkes
Paul Shaw
Alan Stephens
Sylvie Temple
Donna Turnbull

Fabian Watkinson

Photographers

Siobhan Bradshaw
Andy Commons
John Carroll
Diana Foster
Edil Saeed
Iris Watson

All rights reserved. No part of this book may be reproduced in any form or by any electronic or mechanical means, including information storage and retrieval systems, without permission in writing from the publisher, except by reviewers, who may quote brief passages in a review.

ISBN: 978-1-78972-782-1

Printed in UK

Independent Publishing Network

Designed by iDia Ltd

Compiled by the Somers Town History Club

Edited by Professor Esther Leslie

Images reproduced with kind permission and thanks to:

Iain Dungavell photos of Oakshott

Father Paschal Worton, St Mary's Church for portrait of Fr. Basil Jellicoe

Origin for St. Pancras Housing archival footage Photographs from the St. Pancras Housing Improvement Society Collection. courtesy of the Camden Local Studies and Archives Centre at the Holborn Library, 32–38 Theobalds Road, London

Still from film of Father Basil Jellicoe in the Anchor pub, Fox News, courtesy of University of Texas

Key texts

Irene Barclay (1976) 'People Need Roots: The Story of the St. Pancras Housing Association'

John Boughton (2018) 'Municipal Dreams: The Rise and Fall of Council Housing'.

Lynsey Hanley (2017) in 'Estates: An Intimate History, Granta London

'Housing Happenings issues 1961, 1958, no.54. Christmas 1974

Malcolm J. Holmes (1989) 'Somers Town: A Record of Change' London Borough of Camden

Simon Pepper, 'Ossulston Street: Early LCC Experiments in High-Rise Housing, 1925–29' in The London Journal, 7:1, 1981.

With kind help of:

Mayor Of London Culture Seeds

Camden Alive

Diorama

Regent Place

RMT

Camden Alive is part of the Mayor's London Borough of Culture and is a Mayor's Cultural Impact Award winner.

London Borough of Culture is a Mayor of London initiative with support from the City of London Corporation's Charity, City Trust Bridge and Airbnb.

Art below: embroidery created at History Workshop on Social Housing, 2019